Baby Food
POUCHES

Inspiring | Educating | Creating | Entertaining

Brimming with creative inspiration, how-to projects, and useful information to enrich your everyday life, Quarto Knows is a favorite destination for those pursuing their interests and passions. Visit our site and dig deeper with our books into your area of interest: Quarto Creates, Quarto Cooks, Quarto Homes, Quarto Lives, Quarto Drives, Quarto Explores, Quarto Gifts, or Quarto Kids.

First Published in 2018 by Fair Winds Press, an imprint of The Quarto Group, 100 Cummings Center, Suite 265-D, Beverly, MA 01915, USA.
T (978) 282-9590 F (978) 283-2742 QuartoKnows.com

Fair Winds Press titles are also available at discount for retail, wholesale, promotional, and bulk purchase. For details, contact the Special Sales Manager by email at specialsales@quarto.com or by mail at The Quarto Group, Attn: Special Sales Manager, 401 Second Avenue North, Suite 310, Minneapolis, MN 55401, USA.

22 21 20 19 18 1 2 3 4 5

ISBN: 978-1-59233-855-9
Digital edition published in 2018
Content for this book was originally published in the following Fair Winds Press titles: *Baby Food Universe*, *Bountiful Baby Purées*, and *Super Nutrition for Babies*

Library of Congress Cataloging-in-Publication Data available

Recipe development: Gemma Bischoff, R.D.
Photography: Glenn Scott Photography pages 4–5, 13, 14, 20, 23, 35, 45, 70, 90, 130 and cover;
   all others Kelly Pfeiffer
Illustration: Shutterstock

Printed in China

The information in this book is for educational purposes only. It is not intended to replace the advice of a physician or medical practitioner. Please see your health-care provider before beginning any new health program.

* Save money *
* Waste less *
* Make healthy choices *
* Take them anywhere *

101 DIY

Baby Food POUCHES

Incredibly Easy Recipes
for Reusable Pouches

KAWN AL-JABBOURI
WITH ANNI DAULTER,
KELLY GENZLINGER, C.N.C., C.M.T.A. AND
KATHERINE ERLICH, M.D.

FAIR WINDS

CONTENTS

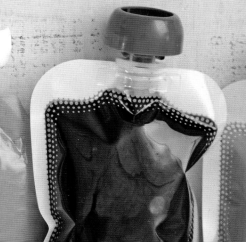

FOREWORD

By Kawn Al-jabbouri, author of *Baby Food Universe*

Being chosen to write the foreword for *101 DIY Baby Food Pouches* was an immense honor given the quality of the authors involved in this amazing new book.

Over the years of building my Instagram page @Babyfooduniverse, it's been a pleasure to be able to share my experiences of healthy eating and talk to many thousands of parents about how to best feed their babies.

Many parents I speak to are looking for a simple solution to feeding their little ones while away from home, and they would prefer to avoid commercial baby food. I continue to make my own baby food pouches for both my children, and I've always recommended others to do the same.

The process of making your own baby food pouches is made easier these days because of the quality of reusable products on the market, which are very inexpensive. Made in advance and frozen at home, they are available at a moment's notice and make last-minute trips outside the house a much

less stressful experience, especially when your baby is first starting solids. For me, it is important that when on the go my children have access to the same nutritious food they have at home and not to rely on store-bought fare. Another advantage of using pouches is in social situations where giving your baby a spoon is often messy and leads to numerous outfit changes. I found that my children mastered feeding themselves with a pouch very quickly and were always excited to find out what was inside. Fillings can be fruit or vegetables, sweet or savory—the possibilities are endless. They become a perfect meal for a busy parent and baby on the move.

On behalf of my fellow authors, we all hope you enjoy the recipes we have lovingly created for you and wish you continued feeding success.

INTRODUCTION

Providing nutritious food for your children is a no-brainer for most parents, but it's not always easy to do when you're running between school, work, play dates, errands, and family commitments. Baby food pouches give you a convenient option on the go that's nearly mess-free, and grocery stores stock an incredible variety of flavors. Unfortunately, it's hard to know what's really in those pouches, and as a one-time-use food item, they produce a lot of waste.

Reusable pouches (of material that does not contain BPA or is the highest quality and low toxicity) are a fantastic alternative that give you full control over what your baby is eating. A few hours of cooking can build a freezer stock of purees that will last for months. And you don't have to stop using pouches when your baby becomes a toddler—even school-age children enjoy pouches in their lunches! Many kids see pouches as treats and will gobble up nearly anything you put in them, which offers you the opportunity to sneak in foods that picky eaters refuse. If pouches are a regular part of your child's early years, you'll save hundreds of dollars by investing in a reusable set and making your own purees.

You may have heard some of the arguments against using pouches for feeding babies. Many of these (environmental impact, questionable freshness, preservatives added to purees) aren't an issue when you make your own purees to fill reusable pouches. One complaint that applies to any type of pouch is that they interfere with the process of learning proper feeding techniques. As long as you use pouches with discretion, there's no need to worry. Reusable pouches are great for quick, healthy meals and snacks on the go. As long as you choose other feeding options for regular meals, baby will still get plenty of messy spoon practice!

GETTING STARTED

There are many different types and sizes of reusable pouches on the market. Look for BPA-free pouches that are durable in the hands of babies and toddlers and won't leak in your diaper bag or lunch box. They should also be easy to fill and clean. There are lots of cute packaging options, but you may prefer clear pouches if you plan to store food in them, allowing you to see if any puree has spoiled or started to mold. The clear pouches are also easiest to clean thoroughly, especially if they have little nooks and crannies that trap bits of food. Dishwasher-safe pouches make clean-up and sterilizing easy.

Pouches also come in multiple sizes. Younger babies will eat less, but consider whether you are investing in pouches that your baby may use for a few years. In that case, you'll want a larger capacity that you can fill with more puree as your baby grows. Some reusable pouch manufacturers offer a filling station to give you an easy way of getting puree into your pouches. Others make a special funnel that's just the right size for pouches.

MAKING PUREES

If you haven't made your own baby food before, don't be overwhelmed! This book is full of puree recipes to give you lots of ideas about what to put into your pouches, and the vast majority of them are very simple. After preparing the ingredients, most recipes instruct you to blend everything together. A food processor is the easiest tool to use for quick and thorough pureeing, as well as easy clean-up. However, a blender or immersion blender will also work—make sure you've blended thoroughly to remove any chunks that could be a choking hazard or clog the opening of the pouch.

In order to make good use of your time, pick a day to cook as many purees as you can. Select your recipes, plan out a grocery trip to get everything you need, and then get cooking! You'll notice that many of the recipes have ingredients in common, so with a little planning, you can use up everything in your grocery bag.

GETTING THE RIGHT CONSISTENCY

For young babies just getting started on solid foods, very runny purees tend to be more palatable. These will work in pouches, but be careful that baby doesn't grab the pouch and give it a squeeze! Even older babies may need thinner purees for some of the thicker, more complex recipes in this book. Some babies have a strong gag reflex and will struggle with food texture, so they need thinner purees for a longer time. You can use breastmilk, formula, homemade stock (beef, chicken, or vegetable), bone broth (see recipe on page 18), or reserved cooking water from steaming to the thin the puree's consistency. Regular drinking water will do the trick, too. Add small amounts (about a teaspoon or less) at a time to avoid going too thin.

Developing brains need lots of fat too. Fat not only builds the brain, but also allows for the absorption and use of fat-soluble vitamins and antioxidants we so covet in healthy fruits and veggies. It is also anti-bacterial, anti-viral, and can therefore support the immune system. Fat is especially suitable for sweet purees (beginning on page 73), given the nutrients of sweet foods are often fat soluble. Fat will also slow down the blood sugar spike from consuming the condensed sugar in cooked fruit. You can add a little fat to any puree without really changing the taste or consistency. Some ideas:

- **Grass-fed butter**
- **Grass-fed ghee**
- **Olive oil**
- **Coconut oil**
- **Avocado oil** (or plain avocado, which will alter the taste)
- **Nut butters** (as long as you've already done an allergy trial)

WHAT YOU'LL NEED

Follow the manufacturer's instructions for filling your reusable pouches. Many open at the bottom for easy filling; some will have a top that pops or screws off. Other pouches come with a convenient filling station that allows you to fill the pouch via the same opening your baby will use to eat from it, which is quick and convenient if you're filling your pouches before freezing

them or serving fresh puree. Most filling stations use a plunger to force the puree through a tube and into the small pouch opening, which also helps to remove air bubbles and fit more puree into your pouch.

STORING PUREES AND PREPARING POUCHES

Once you make your purees, let them cool completely before storing. It's not a bad idea to let them chill in the refrigerator for a few hours, or overnight, before moving them to the freezer. You can freeze purees directly in the reusable pouches, but this will limit the amount of puree you can store at one time to the capacity of your pouches. If you're cooking a lot at one time, portion the puree out into ice cube trays. Freeze the cubes, and then pop them out and store them in labeled bags or containers in your freezer. Regular-sized ice cube trays will work, but you can also purchase trays with smaller cubes that give you more flexibility. Trays with one-inch cubes work really well for this project. Depending on the size of the reusable pouches you've selected, these smaller cubes may make it easier to fill your pouches and combine multiple purees in a single pouch.

When you want to defrost the cubes, you can set them out at room temperature and expect thawed puree in about 30 minutes or less. Then, you fill your pouches and go! Alternatively, you can put the frozen cubes directly into your reusable pouches and let them thaw on the go, but you won't be able to fit as much puree this way. A frozen pouch-full of puree will take longer to thaw than a one-inch cube and can be thawed in a bowl of warm water. Remember, one of the benefits of making your own purees is avoiding preservatives. This means that your purees will spoil faster than commercially processed food and should be kept chilled if not consumed immediately after cooking. Thawing on the go is an easy way to keep a pouch cold without any fuss!

Whatever thawing method you choose, never microwave reusable pouches or purees. Microwaving the pouches can create hot spots that will burn your child as he or she eats. Same with microwaving your frozen puree cubes—you run the risk of introducing heat when you fill the pouch, which will encourage bacteria to grow. Finally, reusable pouches aren't made for the microwave. Like any plastic, their molecules will break down and mix into the food.

You can mix purees with complementary flavors in a single pouch to add even more flavor variety. As with any baby feeding technique, always introduce new ingredients one at a time to check for an allergic reaction.

KITCHEN HYGIENE

Proper kitchen hygiene is a very important part of making home-cooked baby food. While it is not possible to create a completely sterilized or germ-free environment, following these simple steps will help prevent bacterial growth.

1. Wash your hands with soap and water.

2. Wash kitchen utensils properly.

3. Wash all produce thoroughly.

4. Use different cutting boards for different types of food. Never cut produce and meat on the same cutting board.

5. Change kitchen towels often.

6. It is best to store the meal in the refrigerator or freezer immediately after it cools to avoid bacterial growth. (Bacteria grow fast at room temperature.) You can freeze baby food that has been refrigerated for 24 hours, but do not freeze it if it has been in the fridge for longer than that.

7. Do not reheat a meal more than once.

8. Never refreeze food that has been defrosted or reheated.

9. Leftovers from a meal should be thrown away, as food that has been in contact with saliva might be contaminated with bacteria.

ALWAYS BUY ORGANIC:
DIRTY DOZEN (and then some)

1. Strawberries
2. Grapes
3. Apples
4. Celery
5. Peaches
6. Leafy vegetables such as spinach, kale, and salad greens
7. Sweet bell peppers
8. Nectarines
9. Cherries
10. Blueberries
11. Cherry tomatoes
12. Root vegetables such as potatoes, carrots, etc.
13. Pears
14. Cucumbers
15. Wheat
16. Corn
17. Oats
18. Almonds

SAFE TO CONSUME IN NON-ORGANIC FORM: CLEAN 15

1. Onions
2. Avocados
3. Pineapples
4. Mangos
5. Asparagus
6. Sweet peas (frozen)
7. Kiwi
8. Bananas
9. Cabbage
10. Broccoli
11. Papaya
12. Eggplant
13. Cantaloupes
14. Sweet potatoes
15. Watermelon

Introducing your baby to the world of solid foods is a great adventure! But no matter what you do in the early days, almost every kid will go through a picky stage at some point. Reusable pouches work wonderfully for changing up the meal or snack routine, and your homemade purees will ensure your child is getting the good nutrition he or she needs. Whether you're playing at the park, visiting the zoo, taking a long car trip, or out running errands, reusable pouches are a handy and delicious way to keep your little ones nourished.

Have fun!

ORGANIC BONE BROTH

Bone broth is an ideal additive for achieving the perfect consistency of your purees before adding to pouches. It can be used in any recipe that calls for liquid or for any recipe that needs thinning. Real soup, made from bones, is excellent for the digestive system because it contains gelatin, which is uniquely able to stimulate and support digestion, making whatever you eat with it easier to digest. The collagen and cartilage (gristle) in bone broth are even more important to building strong bones than calcium. The minerals obtained from soup stock made with bones are extremely nutritious and in highly absorbable form, resulting in an electrolyte (mineral) solution far superior to any commercially produced, additive-laden, dyed, sugar-spiked beverages such as Pedialyte or Gatorade. Known for generations, across geographies, religions, and ethnicities, broth has the ability to improve and protect digestive, skeletal and joint health.

YIELD

3 quarts (2.8 L)

INGREDIENTS

1 to 2 pounds (455 to 910 g)
soup bones from organic,
grass-fed animals (such
as beef, lamb, or poultry)

2 tablespoons (28 ml) raw
apple cider vinegar

2 chicken feet for extra
gelatin

Sea salt, to taste

Note

The acidity in the water helps
to pull minerals from the bones,
but too much vinegar will alter
the taste of the broth; typically
1 to 2 tablespoons (15 to 30 ml)
to ½ cup (120 ml) of vinegar
is used, depending on the
amount of water.

1. For beef or lamb bones, soak for 1 hour in
   enough water to cover with vinegar to help
   pull the minerals from the bones into the
   consumable liquid. Chicken bones are thin and
   don't need to be presoaked.

2. Add enough water to fill the pot and simmer on
   low for 12 to 24 hours for poultry or 24 to 72 hours
   for beef or lamb (the longer the bones simmer,
   the more minerals and gelatin will be present in
   your stock).

3. Let cool. Add sea salt to taste and to provide
   trace minerals.

4. Serve warm, not hot, to your baby or combine
   with any savory puree.

5. Allow to cool in the refrigerator and then skim off
   the fat that rises and firms as a top layer. (This
   fat can be saved and later used for cooking.)

Storage

- Pour through a mesh strainer into glass storage
  containers or stainless steel ice cube trays as an option
  for freezing individual serving sizes. (If you use plastic ice
  cube trays, ensure broth is room temperature or cooler
  before pouring into the tray.)

- For use within a week or two, place in refrigerator;
  otherwise, freeze. Once defrosted, use within 3 to 4 days.

- When refrigerated, broth should become gelatinous.

SAVORY PUREES

Savory purees in pouches will introduce your baby to a world of new flavors! Some of the stronger flavors may surprise your baby the first time he or she tastes them. Don't give up—for many babies, it takes several tries before they begin to enjoy a new food. Adding breastmilk or formula to the pouch the first time you give a new flavor will help your baby adjust to the new taste. The purees in this chapter start out simple, with just one or two ingredients, and gradually become more complex. It is best to introduce ingredients one at a time before offering pouches with a combination of foods. If you're making pouches for toddlers or older children, look toward the end for more filling combinations.

MASHED AVOCADO

Avocados are a fabulous source of monounsaturated fats and contain the enzyme lipase, which predigests the avocado's fat as it ripens—great for your baby's developing digestive system. Choose a soft (neither super squishy nor hard) Haas avocado with dark brown skin.

YIELD
1¼ cups (213 g)

INGREDIENTS
1 Haas avocado

1. Slice the avocado in half all the way around; then, holding each half in your hands, twist the halves apart. Cut away any brown spots.

2. Remove the pit and scoop the flesh from the peel. Place flesh in a bowl and mash with a fork. Add 1–2 tsp of liquid to desired consistency.

PURE ENGLISH PEAS PUREE

There is nothing like sweet fresh English peas, especially if they are straight from your baby food garden. I know this is somewhat labor intensive, but the difference in taste is incredible. English peas are expensive, so I do suggest throwing them in your garden plot, and when they are ready, your older children can help pick and shell, which is fun and appetizing.

YIELD
1½ cups (338 g)

INGREDIENTS
1 pound (455 g) fresh English peas, shelled

1. Steam peas for 4 to 5 minutes, until they are soft.

2. Reserve the water from the steamer.

3. Blend the peas in a blender until pureed. Add 1 teaspoon (5 ml) of reserved water at a time, if necessary, until desired consistency is achieved.

PURE CARROT PUREE

The primary thing to keep in mind when feeding your baby carrots are the nitrate levels. Nitrates are naturally occurring elements in soil, but when commercial fertilizers are used, they can cause an excess of nitrates to build up in the soil (and surrounding well water) and leech into the plants. Because it's important that young babies not ingest high levels of nitrates, be sure to buy organic carrots or grow your own—particularly if you know your soil is safe.

YIELD

3 cups (750 g)

INGREDIENTS

6 large carrots, peeled and diced

1. Steam the carrots for about 10 minutes or until soft. Reserve the liquid from the steamer.

2. Puree the carrot in a food processor with ½ up (120 ml) of the reserved liquid. Add more liquid as needed to obtain the desired consistency.

PHYTO PARTY VEGGIES IN STOCK

Veggies should be well cooked, soft, and mushy before serving. Cooking in soup is a great way to accomplish this. Ideally, veggies should be consumed with fat or stock since much of their antioxidant nutrition is fat soluble and thus less useful without fat. In addition to soaking up minerals, the veggies will become more digestible.

YIELD
1 cup (250 g)

INGREDIENTS
2–3 carrots
2–3 parsnips
2–3 rutabagas

1. Dice vegetables and cook in stock until they are soft.

2. Drain vegetables, reserving cooking liquid.

3. Mash vegetables with a fork and thin with reserved cooking liquid to desired texture.

ROASTED EGGPLANT PUREE

Eggplant is a delicious delicacy to introduce to your baby. The nutty flavor is unique and offers him or her a nice boost of vitamin C and potassium.

YIELD
1½ cups (375 g)

INGREDIENTS
2 purple globe eggplants,
    cut down the middle
1 tablespoon (15 ml) olive oil

1. Preheat the oven to 350° F (180° C, or gas mark 4).

2. Oil the eggplants and roast for 15 to 20 minutes.

3. Allow to cool and peel off the skin.

4. Place the eggplant in the blender and puree to desired consistency.

SWEET POTATO AND BLACK BEAN PUREE

Protein sources do not always have to be meat. Adding beans to your baby's diet provides variety while ensuring he or she gets some needed protein. This, though, should not be one of the first purees you feed baby, as the protein in the black beans can be harder to digest than other foods. This puree will keep in the freezer for up to three months.

Organic, canned black beans are equally yummy, and make for a quicker option. If you use dried beans, soak them for at least 10 to 12 hours before boiling in fresh water. Sweet potatoes are filled with vitamin A and fiber. Their creamy, sweet, natural taste is highly appealing to most babies.

YIELD
1–2 cups (225–450 g)

INGREDIENTS
1 large sweet potato
½ cup (125 g) dried black beans soaked overnight in water, or (120 g) organic canned black beans

1. Peel and chop the sweet potato.

2. Place the chopped sweet potatoes into a steamer pot. Steam for about 15 minutes or until soft. Reserve the cooking water to use for thinning the puree, if needed.

3. Boil the black beans. If using dried, soaked beans, boil them for at least 30 minutes or until soft. Drain the beans and discard their cooking water.

4. Blend it all. A food processor or blender works best here. Add 1–2 tsp of breastmilk or formula if needed to thin consistency.

Tip
Beans (dry) are most nutritive and least inflammatory if soaked for twenty-four hours prior.

ASPARAGUS, CHICKPEA, AND SWEET POTATO PUREE

This makes a protein-rich, creamy, satisfying baby meal. Asparagus adds a nutty taste, chickpeas create the sustenance, and sweet potato adds sweetness. This puree will keep well in the freezer for up to three months.

From time to time, asparagus can cause little ones to have a little extra wind. It's generally nothing to worry about, but make a mental note in case you notice some unwanted side effects.

YIELD
2–3 cups (450–675 g)

INGREDIENTS
1 large sweet potato

1 handful asparagus, fresh or frozen

1 to 2 tablespoons (10 to 20 g) cooked chickpeas, or (15 to 30 g) canned organic unsalted

1 to 2 tablespoons (10 to 20 g) breastmilk or formula

1. Preheat the oven to 400°F (200°C, or gas mark 6).

2. With a fork, poke holes all over the sweet potato's skin.

3. Place the sweet potato on a baking sheet or in a baking dish and bake for 40 to 45 minutes or until the flesh turns soft and tender when pierced with a fork.

4. Cool and peel the sweet potato.

5. Remove and discard the woody ends of the asparagus. Chop the asparagus into 1-inch (2.5 cm) lengths.

6. Place the chopped asparagus into a steamer pot. Steam for about 15 minutes or until soft.

7. Blend it all. A food processor or blender works best here. Add breastmilk or formula to reach desired consistency.

SWEET POTATO AND KALE

Kale is known as the king of greens for a good reason—it is one of the healthiest vegetables around. Even spinach cannot compare to the number of nutrients that kale provides. To maintain the maximum amount of nutrients, it is recommended that you steam it for 5 minutes.

You can sneak any veggie your little one is refusing to eat, including bitter kale, into his diet if you mask it with sweet potato. This creamy, tasty combo is filled with nutrients and is an excellent source of vitamins A and C, as well as iron. This puree will keep well in the freezer for up to three months.

YIELD
3–4 cups (675–900 g)

INGREDIENTS
2 large kale leaves
3 small sweet potatoes

1. Preheat the oven to 450°F (230°C, or gas mark 8).

2. Remove and discard the kale stems. Chop.

3. Place the chopped kale into a steamer pot. Steam for about 5 minutes or until soft.

4. With a fork, poke holes all over the sweet potatoes' skin.

5. Place the sweet potatoes on a baking sheet or in a baking dish and bake for 40 to 45 minutes or until the flesh turns soft and tender when pierced with a fork.

6. Cool and peel the sweet potato.

7. Blend it all. A food processor or blender works best here.

BROCCOLI, LEEK, AND BASIL PUREE

Fresh aromatics added to baby food freshen up meals and offer fun and unique flavor twists that naturally expand a baby's palate. Basil is a wonderful herb that is traditionally used in many Italian dishes, but it can be easily paired with a wide variety of dishes. It has antibacterial properties and is high in iron.

YIELD

2½ cups (650 g)

INGREDIENTS

1 cup (70 g) broccoli, chopped small

1 small leek, chopped small

1 cup (40 g) fresh chopped basil

1. Steam broccoli and leek for 7 to 10 minutes, until soft. Reserve the water from the steamer.

2. Puree the broccoli, leek, and basil in a blender or food processor. Add 1 teaspoon (5 ml) of reserved water at a time, if necessary, until desired consistency is achieved.

BEET, CARROT, AND CHICKPEA PUREE

This puree is so nutritious, delicious, and colorful. However, the beet component, though a great source of iron, folate, and antioxidants, will have you beaten if it gets on clothes. Have wipes at the ready and definitely leave that white onesie in the dress ___ ___ ___ ___ ll with this combo if you want to add some protein. This puree wil ___ ___ ___ ___ e freezer for up to three months.

YIELD
2–3 cups (450–675 g)

INGREDIENTS
3 carrots
¼ small beetroot
½ cup (82 g) cooked chickpeas, or (120 g) canned organic unsalted

1. Peel and chop the carrots and beet.

2. Place the chopped carrots and beets in a saucepan with water or into a steamer pot. Boil or steam for 15 to 20 minutes or until soft.

3. Blend it all. A food processor or blender works best here.

BUTTERNUT SQUASH, CAULIFLOWER, AND KALE PUREE

Rest assured your baby has munched on a very nourishing meal with this vegetable puree. A simple puree with a very hearty texture is great for batch cooking and leaves plenty of room to add different types of protein. Beef, chicken, turkey, or even fish (such as salmon) can be added to make this into a more satisfying meal. It will keep well in the freezer for up to three months.

YIELD
3–4 cups (675–900 g)

INGREDIENTS
1 small butternut squash
1 large kale leaf
¼ head cauliflower

1. Halve the butternut squash. Remove the seeds and pulp and chop.

2. Remove and discard the kale stem and cauliflower leaves. Chop kale and cauliflower.

3. Place the chopped squash, kale, and cauliflower into a steamer pot. Steam for 15 minutes or until soft.

4. Cool and peel the squash.

5. Blend it all. A food processor or blender works best here.

GREEN BEANS, RED BELL PEPPER, AND SWEET POTATO PUREE

Sweet potatoes are a perfect vehicle to deliver all sorts of other fabulous tastes in a mashed and merry bundle. While this puree does call for steaming, feel free to roast the sweet potatoes and bell peppers in the oven instead. Store it in the refrigerator for up to 24 hours.

YIELD
1–2 cups (225–450 g)

INGREDIENTS
3 medium sweet potatoes
¼ red bell pepper, seeded
1 large handful green beans

1. Peel and chop the potatoes.

2. Trim and chop the green beans.

3. Seed and chop the red bell pepper.

4. Place the chopped sweet potatoes, green beans, and red bell pepper into a steamer pot. Steam for about 15 minutes or until soft. Green beans cook faster, so add them to the steamer 5 minutes after the potatoes and bell pepper.

5. Blend it all. A food processor or blender works best here. Add a few teaspoons of breastmilk, formula, or stock if needed to achieve desired consistency.

GREEN BEANS, BUTTER BEANS, AND PEAR PUREE

Butter, or lima, beans and other legumes contain certain sugars our bodies can't break down and can often cause gassiness. If your baby has a sensitive tummy, you might want to use only half the amount of beans, or wait until your little one is eight months or older to introduce this recipe. This puree will keep well in the freezer for up to three months.

YIELD
1–2 cups (225–450 g)

INGREDIENTS
2 pears
1 handful green beans
¼ cup (47 g) cooked butter (lima) beans, or (60 g) canned organic unsalted

1. Peel, core, and chop the pears.

2. Trim and chop the green beans.

3. Place the chopped pears and green beans into a steamer pot. Steam for 10 to 12 minutes or until soft.

4. Blend it all. Place all the ingredients in a blender, or use an immersion blender, and blend.

MASHED NOT-POTATOES

Since white potatoes are part of the nightshade family—which can cause inflammation—we don't recommend them at an early age. Either taro (a tuber) or cauliflower can be used to make a mashed potato–like side dish without the risk. Part of Polynesian cuisine, taro must be well cooked.

MASHED CAULIFLOWER:

YIELD
1 cup (225 g)

INGREDIENTS
1 crown cauliflower
Butter or ghee to taste
Celtic sea salt to taste

1. Steam the cauliflower until mushy.

2. Drain the water.

3. Puree with the butter or ghee and sea salt until desired consistency.

MASHED TARO:

YIELD
1 cup (225 g)

INGREDIENTS
2 to 4 taro roots
Ghee, butter, or other fat
  to taste
Celtic sea salt to taste

1. Preheat the oven to 300°F (150°C, gas mark 2).

2. Bake the taro for 1 hour. When cool enough to handle, peel. Mash with fat of choice and sea salt.

3. **Optional:** Add coconut milk or grated hard, raw cheese (such as Colby or cheddar).

SAVORY CARROT PUREE

Carrots are sweet and delicious and make a wonderful meal for your baby. You can also add in a little flavor to boost the appeal. Turning this meal into a warm and inviting soup for the rest of your family is the perfect way to usher in the fall.

YIELD

3 cups (750 g)

INGREDIENTS

4 full carrots, peeled and
    diced
1 garlic clove, minced
1 tomato, chopped

1. Steam the carrots and garlic for about 10 minutes or until soft. Reserve the liquid from the steamer.

2. Add the tomato during the last two minutes.

3. Puree the carrot mixture in a food processor with ½ cup (120 ml) of the reserved liquid. Add more liquid as needed to obtain the desired consistency.

BROCCOLI, KALE, COCONUT, AND COUSCOUS

Get those greens in! This puree will keep well in the freezer for up to three months. Do make note that couscous is a grain and contains gluten.

YIELD
1–2 cups (225–450 g)

INGREDIENTS
1 kale leaf, stem removed
4 broccoli florets
½ cup (88 g) couscous
½ teaspoon (2.5 g) coconut butter

1. Chop the kale and broccoli.

2. Place the chopped kale and broccoli into a steamer pot. Steam for about 10 minutes or until soft.

3. Cook the couscous in water according to the package directions.

4. Blend it all. A food processor or blender works best here.

WALNUT, EGG YOLK, AND SWEET POTATO PUREE

This puree is wonderful for neurological and nerve development, and the unusual combination really gives it that wildcard taste factor. True, it isn't common to use egg yolks or walnuts in a baby puree, but isn't it a shame these super omega-3 foods are forgotten? If there are no allergies in the family, explore different foods for your adventurous eater. Store it in the refrigerator for up to 24 hours.

YIELD
1–2 cups (225–450 g)

INGREDIENTS
2 organic, free-range eggs
1 medium-size sweet potato
3 walnuts

1. Hard-boil the eggs. Bring a pot of water to a boil and then slowly add eggs and boil for 10 to 12 minutes.

2. Peel, chop, and boil the sweet potato. Place the chopped sweet potato in a sauce pan with water. Boil for about 15 minutes until tender.

3. Grind the walnuts. Use your blender, or crush them, and be sure to blend all ingredients very well at the end.

4. Peel the eggs.

5. Remove the whites and save for another use.

6. Blend it all (except egg whites). Blend it very well, making sure the walnuts are completely ground to avoid choking hazards. A food processor or blender works best here.

CHICKEN, ASPARAGUS, AND GREEN BEAN PUREE

This is a delicious, savory, and filling meal. If the consistency becomes a bit gluey when pureed because of the potato, add a little liquid. Spice it up with a seasoning of choice if your baby is over eight months of age. This puree will keep well in the freezer for up to three months.

YIELD
1–2 cups (225–450 g)

INGREDIENTS
½ organic boneless, skinless chicken breast
3 asparagus spears
1 handful green beans
2 medium-size white potatoes

1. Dice the chicken.

2. Remove and discard the woody ends of the asparagus. Chop.

3. Trim and chop the green beans.

4. Peel and chop the potatoes.

5. Place the diced chicken and chopped asparagus, green beans, and potatoes into a steamer pot. Steam for about 15 minutes or until the chicken is thoroughly cooked and the vegetables are soft.

6. Blend it all. A food processor or blender works best here. If potatoes become gluey after pureeing, add a small amount of breastmilk or formula to achieve desired consistency.

Tip
Liver or other organ meats can be used in place of chicken.

HUMMUS PUREE

Hummus is a tasty way to get baby some needed protein. This recipe has a great flavor profile for your baby to get accustomed to because it makes a protein-packed lunch for school days when he or she is older. Hummus lends itself well to added flavors, such as nuts, olives, or other vegetables.

YIELD

2 cups (500 g)

INGREDIENTS

1 can (14 ounces or 396 g) garbanzo beans, drained
3 garlic gloves, minced
1 tablespoon (15 ml) olive oil
3 tablespoons (45 ml) lemon juice

Puree all ingredients in blender or food processor until smooth.

CAULIFLOWER, SWEET POTATO, AND GREENS PUREE

Here's another veggie puree that's packed with good nutrition. This puree will keep well in the freezer for up to three months.

YIELD
1–2 cups (225–450 g)

INGREDIENTS
2 kale leaves
2 small sweet potatoes
2 cauliflower florets
1 handful green beans

1. Remove and discard the kale stems and chop.

2. Peel and chop the sweet potato.

3. Trim and chop the green beans.

4. Chop the cauliflower.

5. Place the chopped kale, sweet potatoes, and cauliflower into a steamer pot. Steam for 15 minutes or until soft. You might want to add the kale 5 minutes into steaming, as it cooks faster.

6. Blend it all. A food processor or blender works best here.

CHICKEN, APRICOT, AND RED LENTILS

Meat and vegetable combos can be a tricky affair. However, one tried-and-true combo beloved the world over is chicken and apricot. It is also a double whammy for protein, as both chicken and lentils are rich in this nutrient. This puree will keep well in the freezer for up to three months.

YIELD
- 2–3 cups (450–675 g)

INGREDIENTS

½ organic boneless, skinless chicken breast

5 dried organic apricots, unsulfured

1 teaspoon (5 ml) oil of choice

½ cup (96 g) red lentils, rinsed

1 cup (235 ml) water or coconut milk

1. Chop the chicken and apricots.

2. In a medium pot over medium heat, heat the oil and sauté the chicken until it is cooked through, about 10 minutes. Add the lentils, apricots, and water. Boil for about 15 minutes, stirring occasionally. Add more water if necessary.

3. Blend it all. A food processor or blender works best here.

> **Tip**
> Lentils (dry) are most nutritive and least inflammatory if soaked for nine hours prior.

PASTA, ZUCCHINI, SWEET POTATO, AND CARROT PUREE

This yummy, colorful puree is packed with vegetables and is very satisfying, which makes it a great meal for your baby to sleep on—especially if your little one tends to wake up hungry during the night. You can also add some protein, like beef or chicken, to the meal, which gives it an iron kick, too. This puree will keep well in the freezer for up to three months.

YIELD

2–3 cups (450–675 g)

INGREDIENTS

3 small carrots
1 large sweet potato
½ zucchini
½ cup (53 g) dry whole-grain pasta (optional)

1. Peel and chop the carrots, sweet potato, and zucchini.

2. Place the chopped carrots, sweet potato, and zucchini into a steamer pot. Steam for 15 minutes or until soft.

3. In a small pot over high heat, bring water to a boil and then cook the pasta for about 8 to 9 minutes or until soft. Drain.

4. Blend it all. A food processor or blender works best here.

Note
Consider using a gluten-free brown-rice pasta, like Tinkyada, instead.

ROASTED VEGETABLE MEDLEY PUREE

This is a fun dish because you can play with it depending on what you have in your garden or fridge at the time. Remember that babies like flavor just as much as you do, so don't be shy about introducing your baby to the spices of life. If you can't find yellow Finn potatoes, which have a very creamy, buttery flavor, substitute Yukon Gold.

YIELD
5 cups (1.25 kg)

INGREDIENTS
3 carrots, peeled and
    chopped
3 small yellow Finn
    potatoes, sliced into
    rounds
1 winter squash, halved and
    seeded
1 red onion, chopped
4 garlic gloves, minced

1. Preheat the oven to 350°F (180°C, or gas mark 4).

2. Place the carrots, potatoes, squash halves (face down), red onion, and garlic on a lined parchment baking sheet. Bake vegetables for 30 to 40 minutes, until soft.

3. Scoop the squash from the skin. Transfer squash and all other ingredients to a blender with ½ cup (120 ml) water and puree. Add more water as needed to obtain the desired consistency.

Variation
Liver (ideally organic and grass fed) is worth considering as an additive to many purees. It is the most nutrient-dense food available, with brain-boosting B vitamins, immune-fighting vitamin A, zinc for growth and intelligence, and blood-building iron. It is a lean meat that does not store toxins. Opening capsules of desiccated liver pills into a puree is another way to get some of liver's benefits without cooking it. Boil ½ cup (118 ml) stock and add 3 ounces (85 g or ⅓ cup) cubed liver. Cook for 10 minutes. Drain and puree with other ingredients, adding liquid as needed to reach the desired consistency.

VEGGIE VARIETAL: ZUCCHINI, PARSNIPS, AND CELERY

Carrots, squash, and sweet potatoes are often the first veggies we think of for our babies. While greens and raw and salad vegetables aren't appropriate for a baby's immature digestive system, a few other options can widen his or her palate and increase nutrients. How about zucchini, parsnips, and celery? These antioxidant- and nutrient-rich veggies will help enrich baby's immune and detoxification systems.

YIELD
1½ cups (340 g)

INGREDIENTS
1 zucchini, diced
3 parsnips, diced
2 stalks celery, diced
2–3 cups stock or 2 tablespoons (28 ml) olive oil; or use (28 g) coconut oil, red palm oil, ghee, butter, or (26 g) lard

1. To cook the zucchini, parsnips, and celery, either sauté them in fat, steam, or simmer for 20 to 25 minutes in stock until very soft.

2. Remove the vegetables from the stock and mix with olive oil, coconut oil, red palm oil, ghee, butter, or lard and a pinch of high-quality Celtic sea salt.

3. After steaming, sautéing, or simmering, puree the veggies, thinning with more stock, breastmilk, or formula.

RED LENTIL AND ONION PUREE

Lentils are full of fiber and taste delicious. You can turn this super protein into so many different meals. They are also another unique flavor profile that expands your baby's palate. This recipe is done in the slow cooker, and if you put it on before you go to bed, in the morning you will have a beautiful lentil dish that requires no further preparation.

YIELD
4 cups (1 kg)

INGREDIENTS

2 cups (384 g) red lentils, uncooked
6 cups (1.5 L) vegetable broth
1 small onion, chopped
3 garlic cloves, chopped
1 teaspoon freshly grated ginger
1 teaspoon fresh thyme

Tip
Lentils (dry) are most nutritive and least inflammatory if soaked for nine hours prior.

I. In a slow cooker, combine all the ingredients and mix well.

2. Cook on low for 6 to 8 hours, until the mixture takes on a somewhat creamy texture.

3. Remove from slow cooker and mash lentils thoroughly. If needed, add breastmilk, formula, or broth to achieve desired texture.

Variation

Liver (ideally organic and grass fed) is worth considering as an additive to many purees. Boil ½ cup (118 ml) stock and add 3 ounces (85 g or ⅓ cup) cubed liver. Cook for 10 minutes. Drain and puree with other ingredients, adding liquid as needed to reach the desired consistency.

THAI COCONUT RICE PUREE

This classic Thai dish is tasty and fun. It gives your growing child a chance to try new foods and flavors. If you want to turn this into a textured meal for an older baby or toddler, skip the blending step at the end.

YIELD

2 cups (350 g)

INGREDIENTS

2 cups (475 ml) coconut milk

¼ teaspoon (2.2 g) turmeric

1 cup (200 g) basmati rice, uncooked

1 yellow onion, minced small

1 garlic clove, minced

¼ teaspoon Bragg Liquid Aminos

I. In a medium saucepan, warm the coconut milk and turmeric together. Add the rice, onion, garlic, and liquid aminos. Stir and cover.

2. Bring to a boil, then reduce heat, keeping the lid on and let simmer for about 10 minutes, or until the rice is tender. Be careful not to overcook the rice.

3. Blend it all. A food processor or blender works best here. Add a few teaspoons of breastmilk, formula, or stock if needed to achieve desired consistency.

KIDNEY BEANS, PARSNIP, BEETS, AND BEEF

Beans are a terrific alternative to grains to make a puree more filling. They are also a great source of protein, making them an alternative to meat. They can, however, give babies a little gas, so cumin is added here to help baby's digestion. Don't be frightened if your baby's stools are pink or red after eating beets—while alarming to see in a diaper, this is normal! This puree will keep in the refrigerator for up to 24 hours.

YIELD
2–3 cups (450–675 g)

INGREDIENTS
1 apple
1 large parsnip
1 small white potato
¼ of a beet
½ cup (92 g) dried kidney beans soaked overnight in water, or (128 g) canned organic unsalted
1 tablespoon (15 g) minced beef or diced beef cubes
½ teaspoon ground cumin

1. Peel, core, and chop the apple.

2. Peel and chop the parsnip, potato, and beet.

3. If you are not using canned beans, place the soaked kidney beans in a saucepan with water and boil for 30 to 40 minutes until soft.

4. Place the chopped apple, chopped vegetables, and beef into a steamer pot. Steam until the meat is cooked through and no red or pink remains when you cut into it.

5. Blend it all. A food processor or blender works best here.

Tip
Liver or other organ meats can be used in place of beef.

THYME, BEEF, CARROT, AND SWEET POTATO PUREE

The beef in this meal is a rich source of iron and protein. Offering your baby meats earlier rather than later helps her maintain proper levels of iron, as the stores he or she was born with start to run out around six months old. Use lean beef—the less marbling, the leaner the cut.

YIELD
2–3 cups (450–675 g)

INGREDIENTS
3 small carrots
2 medium-size sweet potatoes
1 clove garlic
½ onion
4 lean beef cubes (about 3 ounces, or 85 g)
1 sprig fresh thyme, or pinch ground thyme (optional)

1. Peel and chop the carrots, sweet potatoes, garlic, and onion.

2. Chop the beef.

3. In a medium pot over high heat, combine all the ingredients. Cover them halfway with water. Boil for about 30 minutes or until the beef is cooked. Cut into a piece of beef to make sure there is no red or pink left inside.

4. Remove and discard the thyme sprig.

5. Blend it all. A food processor or blender works best here. Add a few teaspoons of breastmilk, formula, or stock if needed to achieve desired consistency.

Tip
Liver or other organ meats can be used in place of beef.

PIZZA PARTY PUREE

Who doesn't like a pizza party? They are a great way to come together and share food. This puree makes a great dipping sauce, too!

YIELD

2½ cups (600 g)

INGREDIENTS

1 tablespoon (15 ml) coconut oil

1 medium yellow onion, chopped

1 garlic clove, minced

1 teaspoon fresh oregano

3 carrots, peeled and chopped

2 cups (360 g) cubed Roma tomatoes

½ cup (20 g) fresh basil

1. In a large pot, heat the coconut oil. Add the onion, garlic, oregano, and carrots and sauté until the onions are golden brown and the carrots are soft.

2. Add tomatoes and basil and stew on medium heat until vegetables are softened and flavors are well blended.

3. Put the entire mixture in the blender and hit pulse until you reach the desired consistency.

ROOT VEGETABLE MASH

As great variation of plain old mashed potatoes, this recipe includes plenty of nutrients and flavor. It is hearty and its soft texture and lightly sweet flavor make it a big favorite among kids. For an iron boost, you can add beef to this puree. This puree will keep in the refrigerator for up to 24 hours.

YIELD

2–3 cups (450–675 g)

INGREDIENTS

4 or 5 white potatoes (approximately 1 pound, or 400 g)
3 broccoli florets
2 parsnips
1 large carrot
1 sprig fresh rosemary or thyme (optional)
3 cups (705 ml) water or stock
1 teaspoon (5 g) butter

1. Peel and dice the potatoes, parsnips, and carrot.

2. Chop the broccoli.

3. In a medium pot over high heat, combine the diced potatoes, parsnips, carrot, rosemary (if using), and water. Boil, covered, for about 10 minutes or until all the produce is soft enough to mash easily with a fork.

4. Add the broccoli and boil 10 minutes more.

5. Add butter and mash.

SLOW COOKER BLACK BEANS, ZUCCHINI, AND FETA CHEESE BLEND

Black beans are filled with protein and packed with flavor. When you offer them with a little feta cheese, it deepens the flavor profile and helps your newly chewing baby practice! Making this dish in the slow cooker makes it little work for you; all it takes is a little preplanning.

YIELD
10 cups (2.5 to 3 kg)

INGREDIENTS
1 pound (450 g) fresh black beans, washed and soaked

32 ounces (1 kg) chicken stock

2 bay leaves

1 onion, chopped

2 cloves of garlic, chopped

2 zucchinis, chopped

½ cup (75 g) feta cheese

1. Soak beans in water overnight

2. The next day, drain your beans and place them to your slow cooker. Cover them with chicken stock.

3. Add onion, garlic, zucchini, and feta cheese.

4. Cook overnight (roughly 8 hours) on high.

5. Remove from slow cooker and mash with a fork. Add breastmilk, formula, or other liquid if needed to achieve desired consistency.

Tip
Beans (dry) are most nutritive and least inflammatory if soaked for twenty-four hours prior.

CHICKEN AND RED LENTIL CURRY PUREE

This meal is all about the benefits of blending your little one's food. You can add plenty of nutritious ingredients, and your baby will love it! This is a wonderful meal for your baby to sleep on. If you want to make it even more filling, add ½ cup rice (97.5 g) or quinoa (92 g). If you use canned corn, buy a low-salt version and rinse the corn well before cooking. This puree will keep in the freezer for up to three months.

YIELD

4–5 cups (900–1125 g)

INGREDIENTS

2 carrots
1 small zucchini
½ organic boneless, skinless chicken breast
Olive oil, for sautéing
1 teaspoon (2 g) salt-free curry powder
½ cup (96 g) red lentils, rinsed
1 ear corn, kernels removed, or ½ cup (82 g) frozen or (105 g) canned organic low-salt
1 scallion, chopped
½ cup (65 g) frozen peas

1. Peel and dice the carrots and zucchini.

2. Dice the chicken.

3. In a large pot over medium heat, heat the olive oil and sauté the carrots and zucchini for 7 minutes.

4. Stir in the curry powder. Sauté for 1 minute more.

5. Add the chicken, lentils, corn, and scallion. Keep cooking! Add enough water to cover by about ½ inch (1 cm). If the pot begins to dry out, add more water as needed. Boil for 25 minutes.

6. Add the peas. Boil for 5 minutes more.

7. Blend it all. A food processor or blender works best here.

> **Tip**
> Lentils (dry) are most nutritive and least inflammatory if soaked for nine hours prior.

CHICKEN AND VEGGIE PUREE

As much fun as the winter season brings, there is also the inevitable cold and flu that little ones seem to drag home from all over town. Warm chicken soup is what most mom-doctors order up when this season hits home. When you add in a loving touch, you boost your children's immunity a ton! Love goes a long way.

YIELD
5 cups (1.25 kg)

INGREDIENTS
6 cups (1.5 L) water
1 small chicken (preferably organic)
1 carrot, chopped
1 yellow onion, chopped
1 celery stalk, chopped
2 garlic gloves, minced
2 sprigs fresh thyme
1 large helping of love

1. In a large soup pot, boil water. Add the whole chicken, carrot, yellow onion, celery, garlic, and thyme.

2. Reduce to a simmer and let cook for 35 to 45 minutes, until the chicken is cooked and the meat is falling off of the bone.

3. Let this mixture cool. Strain half of the broth into another bowl and refrigerate for future use.

4. Take the whole chicken out of the pot and pull all of the meat off. Place the meat back into the pot.

5. Transfer the contents of the pot to the blender (working in batches if you need to) and blend to a consistency your baby can handle, adding additional broth as necessary.

6. Don't forget to add the love! (That is the secret ingredient.)

> **Tip**
> Liver or other organ meats can be used in place of chicken.

CHICKEN, VEGGIES, AND LENTILS

This super healthy puree meets all your baby's daily needs for protein, vitamins, and minerals. Great for batch cooking, this is a great winter or fall puree to kick-start your little one's immune system into gear to fight colds. It is so hearty, almost a stew, and the double protein kick from the lentils and chicken give your baby that slow energy release he or she needs. This puree will keep in the freezer for up to three months.

YIELD
4–5 cups (900–1125 g)

INGREDIENTS
1 small Hokkaido pumpkin
  (Substitute: acorn squash)
½ onion
2 small sweet potatoes
1 parsnip
½ organic boneless, skinless
  chicken breast
1 tablespoon (15 ml) olive oil
2 cups (475 ml) chicken
  broth or water
½ cup (96 g) red lentils,
  rinsed

1. Halve the pumpkin. Remove the seeds and strings and chop. If you bought organic, you do not need to peel the Hokkaido, as the skin is edible.

2. Peel the onions, sweet potatoes, and parsnip and chop.

3. Dice the chicken.

4. On a saucepan over medium heat, heat the oil. Sauté the chicken and vegetables for about 10 minutes. Cook the chicken until it is white and no longer pink.

5. Add the chicken broth and boil for 10 minutes.

6. Add the lentils and boil for 10 to 15 minutes.

7. Blend it all. A food processor or blender works best here.

> **Tip**
> Lentils (dry) are most nutritive and least inflammatory if soaked for nine hours prior.

FISH AND PUMPKIN PUREE

Fish is a great addition to any baby or child's diet! When consuming freshwater fish, it is important to know where it came from because of contamination levels in certain areas. You can find out more through your state's health department or Department of Environmental Conservation websites. This puree will keep well in the freezer for up to three months.

YIELD
3–4 cups (675–900 g)

INGREDIENTS
4 medium-size parsnips
½ Hokkaido pumpkin
    (Substitute acorn squash
    if unavailable.)
1 tablespoon (15 ml) oil
1 small whitefish fillet of
    choice, frozen is fine if it is
    good quality and thawed
    before use
½ teaspoon ground cumin
½ teaspoon ground thyme
1½ cups (355 ml) water or
    chicken broth
½ cup (65 g) frozen peas

1. Preheat the oven to 400°F (200°C, or gas mark 6).

2. Peel the parsnips and chop.

3. Remove the seeds and strings from the pumpkin and chop. If you bought organic, you do not need to peel the Hokkaido, as the skin is edible.

4. Place the fish in a baking dish and season with cumin and thyme. Bake for 20 minutes or until cooked.

5. Meanwhile, in a large pot over medium heat, heat the oil and sauté the chopped parsnips and pumpkin for about 2 minutes.

6. Add the water. Boil for 15 minutes.

7. Add the peas. Boil for 5 minutes more.

8. Blend it all. A food processor or blender works best here.

SUPER VEGETABLE AND FISH MEAL

You cannot go wrong with this super-tasty superfood meal! This puree will keep well in the freezer for up to three months.

YIELD
2–3 cups (450–675 g)

INGREDIENTS
1 kale leaf
2 carrots
½ whitefish filet (about 2½ ounces, or 70 g), fresh or frozen
1 tablespoon (15 ml) olive oil
¼ cup (60 ml) water
½ cup (77 g) fresh sweet corn, or canned low-salt, or (140 g) frozen
½ cup (65 g) frozen peas
½ teaspoon (1.25 g) ground cumin

1. Remove and discard the kale stem and chop kale leaves. Chop the carrots and dice the whitefish filet.

2. In a medium pot over medium heat, heat the olive oil and sauté the carrots and kale.

3. Add the water and boil for 10 minutes.

4. Add everything else. Simmer for 15 minutes, adding a little more water if needed.

5. Blend it all. A food processor or blender works best here.

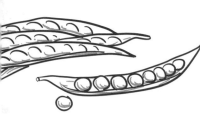

VEGGIE RATATOUILLE

This is a classic dish that gives your baby all kinds of garden goodness in one meal. It's fun to have a tasty dish that uses every leftover vegetable.

YIELD

4 cups (1 kg)

INGREDIENTS

2 tablespoons (30 ml) coconut oil
1 yellow onion, chopped
1 garlic clove, minced
1 teaspoon fresh oregano
2 cups (375 g) cubed Roma tomatoes
1 zucchini, peeled and cubed
1 yellow bell pepper, cubed
1 small purple eggplant, peeled and cubed
½ teaspoon fresh rosemary
½ cup (20 g) fresh basil

1. In a large pot, heat the coconut oil. Add the onion, garlic, and oregano and sauté until lightly browned.

2. Add tomatoes, zucchini, bell pepper, eggplant, rosemary, and basil and stew on medium heat until vegetables are softened and flavors are well blended.

3. Put the entire vegetable medley in the blender and hit pulse until you reached the desired consistency.

SWEET PUREES

Here are lots of food combinations that your little one will love, but don't let the flavor fool you—these sweet purees are full of important vitamins and minerals. The sweet flavor profile is closer to what your baby is used to from breastmilk or formula, so you may not need to add much liquid to these recipes. If you make several fruit purees at once, try mixing complementary flavors in a single pouch. Some of the simpler purees in this section can be mixed with almost any other puree to help alter the consistency or create a flavor profile that's more familiar to baby.

BABY'S FIRST APPLE PUREE

Apple puree is nutritious, easy on baby's tummy, and helps guard against constipation as it is filled with fiber. Apples rarely cause allergic reactions and make a wonderful base for many other purees. While the bulk of the apple's nutrition is in the peel, until your little one is used to a lumpier consistency, it is safer to remove it. If you want to leave the peel on, blend the cooked apples in a food processor to ensure no large, fibrous bits of peel remain. This puree will keep well in the freezer for up to three months and is easy to mix with almost anything else you want to puree and serve in a pouch!

YIELD
3–4 cups (675–900 g)

INGREDIENTS
6 sweet apples

1. Peel, core, and chop the apples.

2. Place the chopped apples into a steamer pot or a saucepan with just enough water to cover. Steam or boil for 10 to 15 minutes or until soft. Add more water if the pot begins to dry out.

3. Blend it all. Use the leftover steamer water or breast milk to thin the consistency, if desired. A food processor or blender works best here.

HOKKAIDO PUMPKIN PUREE

The Hokkaido pumpkin is easy to work with, creamy, and naturally sweet. Its vibrant color makes it a great first food for babies. It is a real vitamin bomb, rich in calcium, magnesium, beta-carotene, and vitamins A, B, and C. It can even help with stomach, kidney, and heart problems. The skin is edible and becomes wonderfully soft when baked. I recommend buying organic Hokkaido pumpkins so you can use the whole squash with confidence. This puree will keep well in the freezer for up to three months.

YIELD
3–4 cups (675–900 g)

INGREDIENTS
1 medium-size Hokkaido pumpkin (substitute acorn squash if unavailable)

1. Preheat the oven to 400°F (200°C, or gas mark 6).

2. Halve the pumpkin. Remove the seeds and strings.

3. Place both halves face down in a baking dish. Add just enough water to cover the bottom of the dish. Bake for 40 to 45 minutes until the pumpkin is soft and tender. Alternatively, you can steam the pumpkin by slicing it into smaller pieces and steaming for 15 minutes, or until soft.

4. Peel the pumpkin. (Note: peeling is difficult and not necessary if you use organic pumpkin.)

5. Blend it all. A food processor or blender works best here.

MASHED BANANA

Bananas' high enzyme content (namely, amylase) means that they can digest themselves and thus, there's less work for your baby's digestive system to do. Choose organic bananas, as sprayed fungicides can reach the fruit inside the porous peel. Also select brown-spotted bananas—they taste the sweetest and are the easiest to digest. Banana puree doesn't freeze well, but this is an easy puree to prepare fresh and give to your baby right away.

YIELD

½ cup (125 g)

INGREDIENTS

1 banana

Mash peeled banana with a fork. Serve immediately.

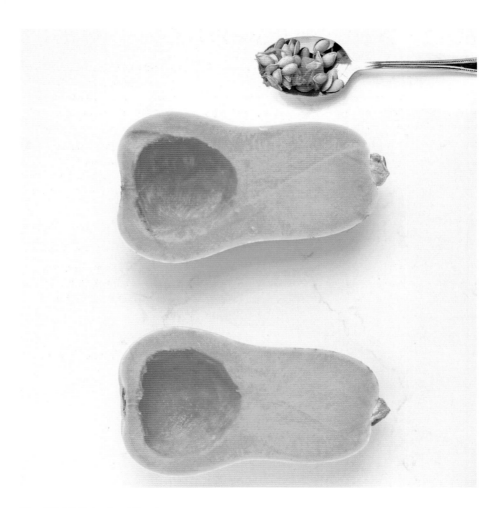

BUTTERNUT SQUASH PUREE

Butternut squash doesn't just taste great, but is also good news for baby's vitamin and mineral intake as it's filled with vitamins A and C and other nutritious goodies, such as beta-carotene. Baking winter squashes, like acorn squash and Hokkaido pumpkin, enhances their naturally sweet flavor. This puree will keep well in the freezer for up to three months.

Be sure to pick a ripe butternut squash. Visually, the squash should be beige all over—the darker, the better, with no green patches. The skin should be matte, not shiny, and free of cuts and blemishes. Feel the squash; it should feel heavy for its size. Tap it gently with your knuckles. You'll hear a hollow sound if it's ripe.

YIELD
3–4 cups (675–900 g)

INGREDIENTS
1 medium butternut squash

I. Preheat the oven to 400°F (200°C, or gas mark 6).

2. Halve the squash. Remove the seeds and pulp.

3. Place both halves face down in a baking dish. Add just enough water to cover the bottom of the dish. Bake for 40 to 45 minutes until the squash is soft and tender.

4. Cool and peel.

5. Blend it all. A food processor or blender works best here.

PURE NECTARINE PUREE

Similar to the peach, this stone fruit is sweet and delicious when in season, and it is a wonderfully easy first food for babies to digest. Babies naturally love this sweet puree, which is a good thing because it's rich in vitamins A and C, among other valuable nutrients.

YIELD

3 cups (750 g)

INGREDIENTS

5 whole nectarines

1. Wash and cut nectarines, leaving skins on.

2. Steam the nectarines for 5 to 7 minutes, or until soft. Reserve the cooking water from the steamer.

3. Transfer the nectarines to a food processor, and add in 2 tablespoons (28 ml) of the reserved water.

4. Puree until desired consistency is achieved.

PURE PEACH PUREE

In the summer, peaches are nature's candy. This stone fruit is sweet and delicious and a great first food for your baby. Peaches are high in vitamins C and A, high in fiber, easy to digest, and considered a low-allergen fruit.

YIELD
3 cups (750 g)

INGREDIENTS
5 whole peaches

1. Wash and cut peaches, leaving skins on.

2. Steam the peaches for 5 to 7 minutes, until soft. Reserve the cooking water from the steamer.

3. Transfer the peaches to a food processor, and add 2 tablespoons (28 ml) of the reserved water.

4. Puree until smooth.

PURE PLUM PUREE

Plums are sweet and full of fiber and vitamin C. They're also a classic baby favorite, and can help move things along if baby becomes constipated.

YIELD
3 cups (750 g)

INGREDIENTS
5 fresh plums, chopped, skins on

1. Steam the plums for 5 to 7 minutes, or until soft. Reserve the liquid from the steamer.

2. Puree the plums with 2 tablespoons (28 ml) of the reserved liquid. Add more liquid as needed to obtain the desired consistency.

SIMPLE PEAR PUREE

Pears rarely cause allergic reactions, are easily digested, and rich in soluble fiber that can help prevent constipation. They are a source of vitamin C, which helps with iron absorption, so they pair well with iron-rich grains such as oatmeal. Freeze for up to 3 months.

YIELD

3–4 cups (675–900 g)

INGREDIENTS

6 ripe pears

1. Peel, core, and chop the pears.

2. Place the chopped pears into a steamer pot. Steam for about 5 minutes or until soft. Add more water if the pot begins to dry out.

3. Mash steamed pears.

SWEET POTATO PUREE

Sweet potato is one of those tastes babies rarely reject. It is an excellent first food because it's easy to digest and rarely causes any allergic reaction. It is filling, high in fiber—which helps prevent constipation—and promotes regularity for a good digestive system. It is also filled with nutrients such as beta-carotene, vitamin C, phosphorous, magnesium, and calcium, to name a few. This puree will keep well in the freezer for up to three months.

YIELD
3–4 cups (675–900 g)

INGREDIENTS
2 medium-size sweet potatoes

1. Preheat the oven to 400°F (200°C, or gas mark 6).

2. With a fork, poke holes all over the sweet potatoes' skin.

3. Place on a baking sheet or in a baking dish and bake for 40 to 45 minutes or until the flesh turns soft and tender when pierced with a fork.

4. Cool and skin. You can remove the skin with your fingers or halve the sweet potato and scoop out the flesh with a spoon.

5. Mash with a fork or immersion blender.

ACORN AND BUTTERNUT SQUASH PUREE

Squash season is always an amazing time of year. It's especially great for babies because these flavors are inviting, easily digestible, and tasty. One squash goes a long way, so this puree is great to use in other ways, which guarantees no waste.

YIELD
4 to 5 cups (1 to 1.25 kg)

INGREDIENTS
1 acorn squash
1 butternut squash

1. Preheat oven to 350°F (180°C, or gas mark 4).

2. Cut both squashes in half and scoop out the seeds.

3. On a lined parchment baking sheet, place the squash halves face down on the sheet and bake for 40 minutes, or until soft.

4. Scoop the squashes from the skins and add to a blender with ½ cup (120 ml) water.

5. Add more water as needed to obtain the desired consistency.

APPLE AND PEAR PUREE

This combination is soft, easy to make, and filled with fiber. Given that pears and apples very common in older kids' diets, it makes sense to introduce them early and offer them at least a few times a week. This puree will keep well in the freezer for up to three months.

YIELD

6 to 8 meals

INGREDIENTS

4 apples
4 pears

1. Peel, core, and chop the fruits.

2. Place the chopped apples and pears into a steamer pot. Steam for 10 minutes or until soft.

3. Blend it all. A food processor or blender works best here.

APPLE AND SWEET POTATO PUREE

This super delicious beginner puree—sweet and vibrant in color—is a big hit with babies. Adding some infant formula or breast milk gives it a creamier flavor that many babies like. This puree will keep well in the freezer for up to three months.

YIELD
4 meals

INGREDIENTS
2 small sweet potatoes
1 apple

1. Peel and chop the sweet potatoes.

2. Peel, core, and chop the apple.

3. Place the chopped sweet potatoes into a steamer pot. Steam for 5 minutes. Add the apple and continue to steam for another 5 to 10 minutes or until soft.

4. Blend it all. A food processor or blender works best here.

APRICOT RASPBERRY PUREE

This is a super-sweet and inviting puree to make for your little sweetie.
As simple as it is, the flavors are just perfect together.

YIELD

1½ cups (375 g)

INGREDIENTS

4 apricots, diced
1½ cups (200 g) raspberries

1. Steam apricots for about 5 minutes. Add the raspberries and steam for an additional 2 minutes.

2. Reserve the water from the steamer.

3. Blend the apricot–raspberry mixture in a blender until pureed. Add 1 teaspoon (5 ml) of reserved water at a time, if necessary, until desired consistency is achieved.

BEETS AND BERRIES PUREE

Beets are so pretty and are full of vitamin B and magnesium. They are an acquired taste, and if you don't want to offer them alone, try this recipe with a little berry lovin' to sweeten the deal.

YIELD

2 cups (500 g)

INGREDIENTS

1 whole beet, peeled and cubed

1 cup (145 g) berries (raspberries, strawberries, or blackberries)

1. Steam the beet for 12 to 15 minutes, until soft.

2. Reserve the liquid from the steamer.

3. Puree the beet and raw berries in a food processor with ¼ cup (60 ml) of the reserved liquid. Add more liquid as needed to obtain the desired consistency.

BUTTERNUT SQUASH AND QUINOA

The chance of quinoa causing an allergic reaction is low. It is a nutritious grain that acts as a natural laxative (like brown rice) and makes a great addition to your little one's diet. It is a source of protein and a great source of vitamins and minerals. This puree will keep well in the freeze for up to three months.

YIELD
3–4 cups (675–900 g)

INGREDIENTS
1 small butternut squash
½ cup (87 g) quinoa

1. Preheat the oven to 400°F (200°C, or gas mark 6).

2. Halve the butternut squash. Remove the seeds and pulp.

3. Place both halves face down in a baking dish. Add just enough water to cover the bottom of the dish. Bake for 40 to 45 minutes until the squash is soft and tender.

4. Wash and cook the quinoa. Quinoa needs a thorough rinse under running water or a soak so its bitterness is washed away. Rub the seeds between your fingers while rinsing. Cook according to the package directions.

5. Cool the squash and peel.

6. Blend it all. A food processor or blender works best here.

CORN PORRIDGE

One of the great things about corn porridge is that it ranks low on the allergy scale and is gluten-free, which makes it a good first food for your little one. It satisfies and can be added to lots of purees to make them more filling. This puree will keep in the refrigerator for 24 hours.

YIELD
1–2 cups (225–450 g)

INGREDIENTS
½ cup (70 g) cornmeal
2 cups (475 ml) water or milk

1. In a saucepan over medium heat, bring the cornmeal and water or milk to a boil, stirring continually.

2. Once it boils, reduce the heat to low and simmer for 2 minutes while stirring.

3. If needed, add breastmilk or formula to thin the porridge until it is the consistency of a creamy soup.

STRAWBERRY AND PLUM PUREE

Strawberries and plums are a dream combination for a baby and for a cook. This sweet combo lends itself to lots of potential dishes, but babies absolutely love this nature's candy. Strawberries are considered a citrus that is also a higher allergen, so waiting until your baby is a little older is better as their digestive tracts get more mature and able to handle more foods. Strawberries and plums are both high in vitamin C, and plums are also high in potassium.

YIELD

2 cups (500 g)

INGREDIENTS

3 plums, peeled and cubed
2 cups (350 g) chopped
  strawberries

I. Steam plums and strawberries together for 5 to 7 minutes, until they are soft. Reserve the water from the steamer.

2. Blend the plum-strawberry mixture in a blender until pureed. Add 1 teaspoon of reserved water at a time, if necessary, until desired consistency is achieved.

HOKKAIDO PUMPKIN AND MANGO PUREE

It's nice to experiment with different fruits and vegetables, such as the Hokkaido pumpkin here, as they all have slightly different flavors—and who doesn't want a baby with a well-developed palate? Hokkaido pumpkin is a great first food as its sweet, creamy taste and texture make it a favorite among babies. It is a wonderful source of calcium, magnesium, phosphorus, potassium, beta-carotene, and vitamins A, B, and C. The peel is edible and delicious once cooked. This puree keeps well in the freezer for up to three months.

YIELD

3–4 cups (675–900 g)

INGREDIENTS

1 small Hokkaido pumpkin
   (Substitute acorn squash
   if unavailable.)
1 ripe mango

1. Halve the pumpkin. Remove the seeds and strings and chop.

2. Peel, pit, and chop the mango.

3. Place the chopped pumpkin into a steamer pot. Steam for 15 minutes or until soft. Alternatively, you can also bake the pumpkin, which enhances its naturally sweet flavor. Steaming retains the maximum nutrients. Once cooled, peel it or if it's organic leave the peel on as it is edible.

4. Blend it all. A food processor or blender works best here.

SWEET POTATO AND BANANA PUREE

This combination is a wonderful first meal for your baby. Both sweet potatoes and bananas are low-allergen foods and easy for your baby to digest. They are also high in vitamin C and potassium.

YIELD
4 cups (1 kg)

INGREDIENTS
1 sweet potato, peeled and diced
2 bananas, peeled and sliced

1. Steam the sweet potato for about 10 minutes or until soft. Reserve the liquid from the steamer.

2. Puree the sweet potato with the bananas in a food processor with ½ (120 ml) cup of the reserved liquid. Add more liquid as needed to obtain the desired consistency.

SWEET POTATO AND PEAR PUREE

Both sweet potatoes and pears are on the low end of the allergen scale, so this combo makes a great first food. You'd be hard pressed to find a baby who won't get into this with some enthusiasm. This puree keeps well in the freezer for up to three months.

YIELD
1–2 cups (225–450 g)

INGREDIENTS
2 ripe pears
1 medium-size sweet potato

1. Preheat the oven to 450°F (230°C, or gas mark 8).

2. Peel, core, and chop the pears.

3. With a fork, poke holes all over the sweet potato's skin.

4. Place the sweet potato on a baking sheet or in a baking dish and bake for 40 to 45 minutes or until the flesh turns soft and tender when pierced with a fork. Cool and peel the sweet potato. Alternatively, you can peel and chop the sweet potato, and then steam it with the pears. Baking will enhance the sweet potato's flavor.

5. Place the chopped pears into a steamer pot. Steam for about 5 minutes or until soft.

6. Blend it all. A food processor or blender works best here.

APPLE, CHICKPEA, AND FLAXSEED PUREE

Flaxseeds are a superfood filled with omega-3 essential fatty acids—the good fats we want more of. They are also filled with fiber, which aids digestion and prevents constipation. However, babies do not benefit unless the flaxseed is finely ground. Use milled or ground flaxseed here. This puree will keep in the freezer for up to three months.

YIELD
2–3 cups (450–675 g)

INGREDIENTS
3 apples
½ cup (82 g) cooked chickpeas, or (120 g) canned organic unsalted
¼ teaspoon ground flaxseed

1. Peel, core, and chop the apples.

2. Place the chopped apples in a steamer pot. Steam for about 10 minutes or until soft.

3. Blend it all. A food processor or blender works best here.

> **Tip**
> Flaxseed is ideally freshly ground right before use and otherwise stored whole (not ground) in the refrigerator given its delicate omaga-3 precursor fatty acids.

APPLE, SQUASH, AND RAISIN PUREE

Both apples and butternut squash are wonderful first foods for baby. They both are easily digestible, high in vitamins A and C, and offer a sweet flavor combination that babies love. Adding the raisins gives this recipe a special touch and an extra boost of fiber.

YIELD
3 cups (750 g)

INGREDIENTS
3 Fuji apples
½ butternut squash
¼ (35 g) cup raisins

1. Peel, core, and cut the apples into 1-inch (2.5 cm) pieces.

2. Peel and cube the butternut squash into 1-inch (2.5 cm) pieces.

3. Steam the apples and butternut squash together for 10 to 12 minutes, or until soft. Add the raisins and steam for 2 additional minutes. Reserve the liquid from the steamer.

4. Puree the apple, butternut squash, and raisins in a food processor with ½ cup (120 ml) of the reserved liquid. Add more liquid as needed to obtain the desired consistency.

PLUM AND FUJI APPLE PUREE

This sweet, dynamic duo is a crowd pleaser. It's the perfect combination of tart and sweet and is a nice starter baby food. It's easy on the tummy and keeps babies wanting more.

YIELD
1½ cups (375 g)

INGREDIENTS
2 plums, peeled and cubed
2 Fuji apples, peeled and cubed

1. Steam plums and apples together for 7 to 9 minutes, until they are soft.

2. Reserve the water from the steamer.

3. Blend the plum-apple mixture in a blender until pureed. Add 1 teaspoon (5 ml) of reserved water at a time, if necessary, until desired consistency is achieved.

APPLES, ZUCCHINI, AND PRUNES

Here's a sweet puree with a veggie punch. The prunes help to relieve constipation. This puree will keep in the freezer for up to three months.

YIELD
3–4 cups (675–900 g)

INGREDIENTS
½ zucchini
3 apples
2 or 3 dried prunes

1. Peel and slice the zucchini.

2. Peel, core, and dice the apples.

3. Chop the prunes.

4. Place the sliced zucchini, diced apples, and chopped prunes into a steamer pot or a saucepan. Steam or boil for 10 to 15 minutes or until soft.

5. Blend it all. A food processor or blender works best here.

BLACKBERRY–BLUEBERRY YOGURT

Yogurt is fabulous for babies, as it is full of live cultures and fats that help with brain development.

YIELD
2 cups (460 g)

INGREDIENTS
½ cup (75 g) whole blueberries

½ cup (75 g) whole blackberries

½ cup (115 g) plain organic and grass-fed yogurt

1. Wash berries with water and steam for 3 to 5 minutes, until the berries are soft.

2. Press steamed berries through a fine sieve to separate seeds, collecting the juice and pulp in a mixing bowl. Be sure to scrape all of the berry pulp off the bottom of the sieve.

3. Reserve the water from the steamer.

4. Blend the juice and pulp mixture in a blender until pureed. Add 1 teaspoon (5 ml) of reserved water at a time, if necessary, until desired consistency is achieved.

5. Transfer the berry mixture to a mixing bowl, add the yogurt, and whisk until fully combined.

> **Tip**
> When choosing yogurt, look for "live" or "active" cultures.

BLUEBERRY, RAISIN, AND ALMOND PUREE

Blueberries are a super antioxidant, raisins are high in iron, and this recipe has the added bonus of almond protein. The alluring, bright-purple color of this recipe, combined with its great taste, make this one a winner with most babies right out of the gate.

YIELD
1½ cups (375 g)

INGREDIENTS
2 cups (300 g) blueberries
¼ cup (36 g) raisins
1 tablespoon (6 g) ground
  almonds

1. Wash berries with water and steam with raisins for 3 to 5 minutes, until the berries are soft.

2. Reserve the water from the steamer.

3. Blend the blueberry-raisin mixture in a blender until pureed. Add 1 teaspoon of reserved water at a time, if necessary, until desired consistency is achieved.

4. Add in ground almonds and mix together.

CHICKEN AND APPLE PUREE

Chicken can be hard to introduce on its own, as many babies initially dislike the flavor. If you gradually introduce it in combinations like this, which give it a bit more of a moist texture, your little one will love it in no time. Chicken goes equally well with fruits or vegetables, giving you endless serving possibilities. The darker thigh and leg meat is richer in iron, so if your baby was born prematurely or suffers with low iron, these are good to use instead of breast or wing meat. This puree keeps well in the freezer for up to three months.

YIELD
2–3 cups (450–675 g)

INGREDIENTS
1 apple
¼ small organic boneless skinless chicken breast

1. Peel, core, and dice the apple.
2. Chop the chicken.
3. In a saucepan over medium heat, heat a small amount of oil and sauté the chicken breast for 5 minutes or until it is no longer pink.
4. Add the diced apple and water.
5. Boil for 10 minutes until everything is cooked.
6. Blend it all. A food processor or blender works best here.

Tip
Liver or other organ meats can be used in place of chicken.

CARROT, APPLE, AND POMEGRANATE PUREE

Pomegranate is a super healthy and delicious fruit with tons of antioxidants, vitamins like A, C, E, and K, and folic acids. It also helps the body absorb iron, and that is just to name a few of its benefits. The seeds are hard and can become sharp when blended, so pass the puree through a sieve to strain any remaining seeds and seed bits. This puree keeps well in the freezer for up to three months.

YIELD
3–4 cups (675–900 g)

INGREDIENTS
1 sweet apple
4 small carrots
½ cup (187 g) pomegranate seeds

1. Peel, core, and chop the apple.

2. Peel and chop the carrots.

3. Place the chopped carrots into a steamer pot. Steam for 5 minutes. Add the apple and steam for 10 minutes more or until soft.

4. Blend it all. A food processor or blender works best here.

5. Pour the puree through a sieve and make sure there are no remaining pomegranate seeds.

CREAMY MILLET PORRIDGE

Millet satisfies a baby's appetite well into the morning. It is also one of the least allergenic grains, which makes it a great first food, especially if your baby is ready for solid food before the age of six months. Millet is gluten free, nutritious, easily digested, and versatile. This puree keeps in the refrigerator for 24 hours. Add a fruit puree to the pouch for more flavor and added nutrients.

YIELD
1–2 cups (225–450 g)

INGREDIENTS
½ cup (100 g) millet, ground in the blender for a softer texture

1½ cups (355 ml) water, or milk

1 teaspoon (5 g) unsalted butter

1. Boil the millet and water. Stir for about 7 minutes until it reaches a porridge-like consistency and large bubbles form.

2. Remove from the heat and add the butter.

KALE, BANANA, AND HEMP SEED PUREE

Kale is one of the healthiest foods around, super high in antioxidants, and, when combined with yummy bananas and protein-packed hemp seed, it makes for a winning baby puree. Hemp seed has the most essential fatty and amino acids of any plant resource and is the most easily digestible. It is becoming mainstream and easily accessible. You should be able to buy it at your local health food grocer or online.

YIELD

2 cups (500 g)

INGREDIENTS

2 cups (60 g) kale
1 banana
¼ cup (35 g) hemp seeds, ground in coffee grinder

1. Wash the kale and cut into pieces.

2. Steam the kale for 5 to 7 minutes, or until soft. Reserve the liquid from the steamer.

3. Transfer the kale to a food processor.

4. Add in banana, ¼ cup (60 ml) of the reserved liquid, and ground hemp seeds.

5. Puree until smooth. Continue to add the reserved liquid in scant 2 tablespoons (28 ml) increments until the puree reaches your desired consistency.

KIWI, BANANA, AND AVOCADO PUREE

Kiwi can be an unusual taste for some babies, so add it sparingly the first few times it's introduced. It is also acidic; if your baby has a sensitive tummy and a tendency to get diaper rashes, you may want to wait until ten to twelve months to serve this fruit. This puree will keep in the refrigerator for 24 hours; it will brown but is still edible.

YIELD
2–3 cups (450–675 g)

INGREDIENTS
1 large banana
1 ripe kiwi
1 ripe avocado

1. Peel and slice the banana and kiwi.

2. Pit the avocado. Peel and chop.

3. Blend it all. A food processor or blender works best here.

PEAR, BANANA, AND NECTARINE PUREE

This fruity puree has lots of yummy flavor and vitamins. It will keep well in the freezer for up to three months.

YIELD
3–4 cups (675–900 g)

INGREDIENTS
2 ripe pears
1 ripe nectarine
1 ripe banana

1. Peel, core, and chop the pears.

2. Peel, pit, and chop the nectarine.

3. Peel and slice the banana.

4. Blend it all. A food processor or blender works best here.

OATMEAL PORRIDGE

Oats are a wholesome food high in calcium, soluble fiber, and iron—and perfect for little growing bodies. They aid digestion, can improve the immune system, and are rich in vitamins and minerals. They are also much easier to digest than rice and are one of the least likely grains to cause an allergic reaction in babies. This puree will keep in the refrigerator for 24 hours.

YIELD
1 to 2 cups (225–450 g)

INGREDIENTS
½ cup (40 g) oats
1½ cups (355 ml) water, breastmilk, or formula
1 teaspoon (5 g) unsalted butter

1. Grind the oats to a fine powder in a food processor or blender.

2. In a small or medium saucepan, stir together the oats and liquid. Break up any lumps.

3. Heat on medium heat while stirring until it reaches a thick consistency and large bubbles form.

4. Add water, breastmilk, or formula to reach the desired consistency. You can also mix in a fruit puree for extra flavor.

Tip
Oats are most nutritive and least inflammatory if soaked for nine hours prior.

PERSIMMON, BERRY, AND MINT PUREE

Persimmons are so pretty with their gorgeous orange skin, and they are the perfect combination of tart and sweet. They look somewhat like tomatoes. They are high in vitamin C and are a great source of fiber.

The two most commonly available types of persimmons are Hachiya and Fuyu. Hachiya persimmons are larger and should not be eaten until very ripe (soft to the touch and almost to the point of mushy). Fuyu persimmons are smaller and more tomato-shaped, and may be eaten while still a bit firm.

YIELD

3 cups (750 g)

INGREDIENTS

3 persimmons, peeled
   chopped
2 cups (250 g) chopped
   strawberries or raspberries
¼ cup (24 g) chopped fresh
   mint

1. Steam persimmons for about 8 minutes until soft. Add the strawberries and steam for 2 more minutes. Reserve the water from the steamer.

2. Puree the mixture in a blender with the mint. Add 1 teaspoon (5 ml) of reserved water at a time, if necessary, until desired consistency is achieved.

PUREED PEACHES AND APRICOTS

Nature provides abundant flavor and natural sweetness in apricots and peaches! Mixing a little yogurt or kefir into the pouch with this puree is delicious and will also help digestion.

YIELD
1½ cups (384 g)

INGREDIENTS
2 peaches, peeled, pitted, and chopped
3 apricots, peeled, pitted, and chopped
Ghee or coconut oil

1. Cook the fruit in the fat over low heat until very soft.

2. Puree fruit and thin to desired consistency with mom's milk or homemade formula.

PUMPKIN, APRICOT, AND DATE PUREE

This creamy, vibrant puree is nutritious and full of fiber. It is also perfect for babies who prefer sweet over savory. Babies are different, and their tastes change like the wind. This puree will keep well in the freezer for up to three months.

YIELD
3–4 cups (675–900 g)

INGREDIENTS
2 ripe apricots (not sour)
½ Hokkaido pumpkin
(Substitute acorn squash if unavailable)
3–7 soft pitted dates for sweetness

1. Place the apricots in a saucepan with water and boil for 1 minute.

2. Cool, peel, pit, and chop the apricots.

3. Remove the seeds and strings from the pumpkin and chop.

4. Place the chopped pumpkin into a steamer pot. Steam for about 15 minutes or until soft. Once cooled, you can peel it or leave the skin on if you use organic, as it is edible.

5. Blend it all. A food processor or blender works best here.

RAW MANGO, PAPAYA, AND COCONUT PUREE

Babies need a lot of iron, and mangoes are full of not only iron, but antioxidants as well. Combine them with juicy papaya (which is great for digestion) and coconut (which is high in the omega-6 fatty acids that help with brain development), and this becomes a tropical treat worth gobbling up.

YIELD
2 cups (490 g)

INGREDIENTS
1 whole mango
½ papaya
¼ cup (20 g) fresh coconut
  flakes

1. Peel and cut mango and papaya into chunks.

2. In a blender or food processor, combine mango, papaya, and coconut flakes and blend to desired consistency.

SPINACH, PINEAPPLE, AND PLAIN YOGURT PUREE

Spinach is packed with protein, antioxidants, and essential vitamins. It loses its nutritional punch after about a week after being picked, so this is a great veggie to grow yourself or buy fresh from a farmer's market. No need to steam this recipe, just pop in all in the blender and hit the puree button.

YIELD

3 cups (750 g)

INGREDIENTS

1½ cups (45 g) spinach leaves, packed

1 whole pineapple, outside cut off and chopped into chunks

1½ cups (345 g) plain organic and grass-fed yogurt

Blend the spinach, pineapple, and yogurt together in a blender until desired consistency is achieved.

> **Tip**
> When choosing yogurt, look for "live" or "active" cultures.

RED CABBAGE, APPLE, AND BANANA PUREE

Have you ever heard of red cabbage in a puree? While it is not an obvious choice, it certainly adds a distinct flavor and a beautiful purple color. While green cabbage is the variety most commonly eaten, it is actually red cabbage that comes out on top regarding nutrition. Its vibrant color indicates its rich abundance of antioxidants. If you want to raise an adventurous eater, be brave and try a few twists and turns along the way—and this turn is absolutely great. This puree will keep well in the freezer for up to three months.

YIELD
2–3 cups (450–675 g)

INGREDIENTS
2 sweet apples
1 cup (90 g) chopped red cabbage
1 banana

1. Peel, core, and chop the apples.

2. Place the chopped red cabbage and apples into a steamer pot. Steam for about 10 minutes or until soft.

3. Strain the steamed red cabbage and apples into a bowl. Add the peeled and sliced banana.

4. Blend it all. A food processor or blender works best here.

RED LENTIL, APPLE, AND SWEET POTATO PUREE

Lentils are a great source of protein and iron, and they are high in fiber. They are especially good if you decide not to feed your baby a lot of meat or if she does not like the taste of meat and you need a substitute. However, if you desire to add meat, chicken and turkey go well with this combo.

There are different types of lentils; some cook faster and smoother than others, so read the package directions. Split red lentils cook much faster than whole ones, for example. This puree will keep well in the freezer for up to three months.

YIELD
2–3 cups (450–675 g)

INGREDIENTS
2 apples
1 large sweet potato
¼ cup (48 g) red lentils, rinsed

1. Peel, core, and chop the apples.

2. Peel and chop the sweet potato.

3. Place the chopped sweet potato into a steamer pot. Steam for 10 minutes. Add the apple and steam for 5 minutes more or until soft.

4. Cook the lentils, following the package directions.

5. Blend it all, adding breastmilk or formula as needed to thin the consistency. A food processor or blender works best here.

Tip
Lentils (dry) are most nutritive and least inflammatory if soaked for nine hours prior.

STRAWBERRY, FIG, AND BANANA PUREE

Figs are delicious! They may seem somewhat exotic, but they are just a simple fruit that many folks don't know what to do with. They have a natural, sticky sweetness that is somewhat nutty in flavor and are high in potassium and fiber. They grow on trees and are part of the Mulberry family. You can make this recipe with dried figs, but they are smaller, so use six instead of four.

YIELD

2 cups (500 g)

INGREDIENTS

2 cups (350 g) chopped strawberries
4 fresh figs, halved
2 bananas, peeled and sliced

1. Steam strawberries and figs together for 3 minutes, until they are soft.

2. Reserve the water from the steamer.

3. Blend the strawberry–fig mixture with the bananas in a blender until pureed.

4. Add 1 teaspoon (5 ml) of reserved water at a time, if necessary, until desired consistency is achieved.

BANANA, ALMOND BUTTER, AND FLAX PUREE

This is a fun way to give your baby protein. Almond butter is super easy to make from scratch as well, if you are motivated. Just grind almonds in a food processor until they turn into a paste, and then eventually almond butter. That's it!

YIELD
2 cups (500 g)

INGREDIENTS
3 bananas, peeled and
   sliced
½ cup (130 g) almond butter
1 cup (230 g) of plain
   organic and grass-fed
   yogurt
1 tablespoon (8 g) ground
   flaxseed

Blend the bananas, almond butter, yogurt, and flaxseed together in a blender until desired consistency is achieved.

> **Tip**
> Flaxseed is ideally freshly ground right before use and otherwise stored whole (not ground) in the refrigerator given its delicate omega-3 precursor fatty acids.

ZUCCHINI, CARROT, AND FIG PUREE

This summer puree bursts with flavor and color. Figs have many health benefits for infants, such as boosting the immune system, aiding digestion, and protecting the liver. They are also a good source of vitamins A, E, and K, as well as the minerals calcium, potassium, and manganese, and they are a great source of dietary fiber. This puree will keep well in the freezer for up to three months. If your baby is over eight months, add a pinch of cinnamon to give this puree a boost of flavor.

YIELD
2–3 cups (450–675 g)

INGREDIENTS
3 ripe fresh figs
3 carrots
½ zucchini

1. Peel and chop the figs, carrots, and zucchini.

2. Place the chopped carrots into a steamer pot and steam. After about 8 minutes, add the zucchini to the steamer pot. Steam for another 8 minutes or until both vegetables are soft.

3. Blend it all. A food processor or blender works best here.

CHICKPEA, BANANA, AND MILLET PUREE

This is like a baby version of hummus! The chickpeas provide a great, slow-release energy and the millet gives a kick of carbs, which are rounded off nicely with the sweetness of banana. This puree will keep in the refrigerator for 24 hours; it will brown but is still edible.

YIELD
1–2 cups (225–450 g)

INGREDIENTS
2 tablespoons (25 g) millet
¾ cup (175 ml) water
2 tablespoons (20 g) cooked chickpeas, or (30 g) canned organic unsalted
1 large ripe banana

1. In a saucepan over medium-high heat, bring the millet and water to a boil. Stir for about 7 minutes until it reaches a porridge-like consistency and large bubbles form.

2. Peel and slice the banana.

3. Add all ingredients and blend. A food processor or blender works best here.

PEAR WITH RYE BREAD PUREE

This is a satisfying, fiber-packed baby meal. The rye bread contains the highest level of bran and provides the most satiety of any bread. It improves digestion and relieves constipation as it is rich in fiber. Just be sure to look for a loaf that has only natural ingredients. Be aware that rye does contain gluten. Add infant formula or breast milk to the puree for a creamier flavor. This puree will keep in the freezer for up to three months.

YIELD
2–3 cups (450–675 g)

INGREDIENTS
1 slice seedless rye bread
(or with seeds, but blend
it well)
2 cups (475 ml) water,
or milk
4 ripe pears
1 teaspoon (5 g) butter

1. Soak the rye bread in the water for 15 minutes. Break it apart with a fork.

2. Peel, core, and chop the pears.

3. Place the chopped pears into a steamer pot. Steam for 5 to 7 minutes or until soft.

4. Blend it all. Blend everything—including the boiling water—until you've reached the desired consistency. A food processor or blender works best here.

PLUM, APPLE, MINT, AND YOGURT PUREE

This puree will keep well in the freezer for up to three months.

YIELD
1–2 cups (225–450 g)

INGREDIENTS
1 sweet apple

3 very ripe plums

4 fresh mint leaves

1 tablespoon (15 g) organic and grass-fed yogurt

1. Peel, core, and chop the apple.

2. Place the chopped apple into a steamer pot. Steam for 10 minutes or until soft.

3. Boil the plums for 1 minute.

4. Cool the plums; remove the peel and pit.

5. Blend it all. A food processor or blender works best here.

Tip
When choosing yogurt, look for "live" or "active" cultures.

SPICED APPLE, PEAR, AND RAISIN PUREE

This is a lovely, spiced-up version of an old classic that even adults will enjoy as a side dish. If your baby is under eight months, omit the cinnamon.

YIELD

3 cups (750 g)

INGREDIENTS

3 Fuji apples, peeled and cubed

3 Bartlett pears, peeled and cubed

1 teaspoon cinnamon

¼ cup (38 g) to ½ cup (75 g) raisins for sweetness

1. Peel, core, and cut the apples and pears into 1-inch (2.5 cm) pieces.

2. Sprinkle cinnamon overs the apples and pears and steam for 8 to 10 minutes, or until soft.

3. Add in the raisins and steam for 2 additional minutes. Reserve the liquid from the steamer.

4. Puree the apple, pears, and raisins in a food processor with ½ cup (120 ml) of the reserved liquid. Add more liquid as needed to obtain the desired consistency.

SPINACH, KALE, AND BANANA PUREE

This puree is packed with nutrition, and the added sweet kick of the banana makes this a pleasing bite for any baby. Spinach and kale are super foods and contain protein and iron. Getting your kids hooked on greens is the way to go, so try this one at least once a week. For another twist, try adding some apple or pear puree to the pouch.

YIELD

2 cups (500 g)

INGREDIENTS

1 cup (30 g) spinach leaves, packed

1 cup (30 g) kale leaves, chopped and packed, stems removed

2 bananas, peeled and sliced

1. Steam spinach and kale together for 3 minutes, until they are soft.

2. Reserve the water from the steamer.

3. Blend the spinach and kale mixture in a blender with the banana slices until pureed. Add 1 teaspoon (5 ml) of reserved water at a time, if necessary, until desired consistency is achieved.

STRAWBERRY, PEACH, PINEAPPLE, AND POMEGRANATE PUREE

The tropical flavors of this puree mixture are loved by all babies. It's super high in antioxidants and has a sweet and tart flavor profile. Make this recipe toward the very end of the summer, when pomegranates are just beginning to come into season (which extends through fall), and you will be able to grab all the natural sweetness from each fruit.

YIELD
4 cups (980 g)

INGREDIENTS
2 cups (350 g) chopped strawberries
2 cups (300 g) chopped peaches (skin on is fine)
1 small pineapple, skinned and chopped into chunks
1 cup (175 g) fresh pomegranate seeds

Combine all ingredients in a blender and puree until well blended. If desired, add in 1 teaspoon of water at time to get the puree to a smoother consistency.

AVOCADO, CHICKPEA, PEAR, AND FLAXSEED PUREE

The avocado, chickpeas, and pear taste wonderful together, and the flaxseed gives this meal a kick of omega-3 fatty acids. Flaxseed is also a high-fiber superfood that works as a natural laxative. Make sure the flaxseed is ground or milled so your baby can benefit from its wonderful nutrients. This puree will keep in the refrigerator for 24 hours.

YIELD
1–2 cups (225–450 g)

INGREDIENTS
3 ripe pears
½ ripe avocado
1 tablespoon (10 g) cooked chickpeas, or (15 g) canned organic unsalted
4 fresh basil leaves (optional)
½ teaspoon (1 g) ground flaxseed (optional)

1. Peel, core, and chop the pears.
2. Pit the avocado. Peel and chop.
3. Blend it all. A food processor or blender works best here.

Tip
Flaxseed is ideally freshly ground right before use and otherwise stored whole (not ground) in the refrigerator given its delicate omega-3 precursor fatty acids.

MILD COCONUT AND PAPAYA CURRY PUREE

After the initial stage of weaning is done and baby is eating happily, it is the perfect time to look into spicing things up. The coconut butter here gives the puree a boost of flavor.

YIELD

1–2 cups (225–450 g)

INGREDIENTS

2 small sweet potatoes
¼ ripe papaya, sliced (no seeds)
⅓ cup (80 ml) coconut milk
¼ teaspoon salt-free curry powder
1 teaspoon (5 ml) coconut butter, or other fat

1. Preheat the oven to 425°F (220°C, or gas mark 7).

2. Wash and dry the sweet potatoes. With a fork, poke holes all over the sweet potatoes' skin.

3. Place the sweet potatoes on a baking sheet or in a baking dish and bake for 40 to 45 minutes or until the flesh turns soft and tender when pierced with a fork.

4. Cool and peel the sweet potatoes.

5. Blend it all. A food processor or blender works best here.

BABY'S SUNSHINE QUINOA MASH

The benefits of quinoa are endless! It's such a nutritious grain, packed with fiber, calcium, iron, and folate. For extra spice, add a pinch of curry powder or cinnamon. This puree will keep well in the freezer for up to three months.

YIELD
2–3 cups (450–675 g)

INGREDIENTS
2 large carrots
2 small sweet potatoes
1 large parsnip
2 tablespoons (23 g) quinoa

1. Peel and chop the carrots, sweet potatoes, and parsnip.

2. Place the chopped carrots, sweet potatoes, and parsnip into a steamer pot. Steam until soft.

3. Quinoa needs a thorough rinse under running water or a soak so its bitterness is washed away. Rub the seeds between your fingers while rinsing. Cook according to the package directions.

4. Blend it all. A food processor or blender works best here.

PURE PUMPKIN RASPBERRY PUREE

Pumpkins are rich in vitamin A and fiber and can be used for many things during the fall. Most popular is the pumpkin pie of course, and while those are super tasty, there are a wide variety of uses for pumpkin. This is a great puree for baby because of its nutty flavors and high nutritional content, but turn leftover puree into pancakes, and you have a winner for everyone.

YIELD

4 to 5 cups (1 to 1.25 kg)

INGREDIENTS

1 small baking pumpkin, seeded
1 teaspoon olive oil
½ cup (120 ml) water
1 cup (125 g) fresh raspberries
1 banana

1. Preheat the oven to 350°F (180°C, or gas mark 4).

2. Cut the pumpkin in half and scoop out the seeds. Brush olive oil on the pumpkin flesh.

3. On a lined parchment baking sheet, place the pumpkins halves flesh side down on the sheet. Bake for 40 minutes, or until soft.

4. Scoop the pumpkin flesh from the skin and add to a blender with ½ cup (120 ml) water and raspberries.

5. Add banana to the blender and puree.

6. Add water as needed to obtain the desired consistency.

QUINOA, APPLE, DATES, AND CINNAMON PUREE

This is a wonderful puree to start your day with, and your entire home will smell like cinnamon. This is a definite favorite superfood meal and will keep well in the freezer for up to three months. Omit the cinnamon if your baby is under eight months.

YIELD
2–3 cups (450–675 g)

INGREDIENTS
¼ cup (43 g) quinoa
1 apple
4 to 6 soft pitted dates
1 ripe banana
½ teaspoon (1 g) ground cinnamon (omit for babies under eight months)

1. Quinoa needs a thorough rinse under running water or a soak so its bitterness is washed away. Rub the seeds between your fingers while rinsing. Cook according to the package directions.

2. Peel and core the apple. Chop the apple and dates.

3. Add the dates and apple to the quinoa. Boil for 15 to 20 minutes. Add more water if needed.

4. Peel and slice the banana.

5. Blend it all. A food processor or blender works best here.

VANILLA, STRAWBERRY, AND BROWN RICE PUREE

Strawberries are rich in vitamin C, and they are a very good source of dietary fiber. This puree will keep well in the freezer for up to three months.

YIELD

2–3 cups (450–675 g)

INGREDIENTS

2 large carrots

5 fresh strawberries

1 tablespoon (12 g) cooked brown rice, or (10 g) white rice

¼ teaspoon (1 g) vanilla powder, or 1 vanilla bean split and scraped

1. Peel and chop the carrots.

2. Place the chopped carrots into a steamer pot. Steam for 15 minutes or until soft.

3. Blend all ingredients together. A food processor or blender works best here.

GINGER-SPICED PUMPKIN PUREE

Pumpkin is so packed with vitamins that getting babies hooked on it is a great accomplishment—and an easy thing to do when you blend it with a little spice. So many pumpkins go to waste during the fall because folks don't think to cook them up, but you should! Use as many as you can when they are ripe and at their best.

YIELD

4 to 5 cups (1 to 1.25 kg)

INGREDIENTS

1 small baking pumpkin
1 teaspoon (5 ml) olive oil
½ cup (120 ml) water
1 teaspoon ground ginger
½ teaspoon cinnamon
½ teaspoon ground nutmeg

1. Preheat the oven to 350°F (180°C).

2. Cut the pumpkin in half and scoop out the seeds. (Save the seeds to roast for a yummy snack for you!) Brush olive oil on the pumpkin flesh.

3. On a baking sheet lined with parchment, place the pumpkins halves flesh side down. Bake for 40 minutes, or until soft.

4. When cool enough to handle, scoop the pumpkin flesh from the skin and add to a blender with water and spices.

5. Puree until smooth. Add water as needed to obtain the desired consistency.

MINTY QUINOA, RASPBERRY, AND COCONUT PORRIDGE

Here's a yummy and refreshing treat that will fill your baby's belly, too! This puree keeps well in the freezer for up to three months.

YIELD
2–3 cups (450–675 g)

INGREDIENTS
2 tablespoons (22 g) quinoa
1 cup (235 ml) water
10 fresh raspberries
½ ripe banana
4 or 5 fresh mint leaves
   (optional)
¼ cup (60 ml) coconut milk

1. Quinoa needs a thorough rinse or a soak so its bitterness is washed away. Rub the seeds between your fingers while rinsing. Cook according to the package directions.

2. Peel and slice the banana.

3. Blend it all. A food processor or blender works best here.

QUINOA, APPLE, RAISINS, AND PEAR PUREE

Quinoa is rich in protein and a great source of vitamins, minerals, and antioxidants. Its high fiber content acts as a natural laxative for your little one, which makes it a good meal for constipated babies. This puree will keep well in the freezer for up to three months.

YIELD

2–3 cups (450–675 g)

INGREDIENTS

½ cup (87 g) quinoa
3 ripe pears
2 sweet apples
¼ cup (35 g) raisins
2 cups (475 ml) water

1. Quinoa needs a thorough rinse under running water or a soak so its bitterness is washed away. Rub the seeds between your fingers while rinsing.

2. Peel, core, and chop the pears and apples.

3. Place the quinoa, pears, apples, and raisins in a saucepan with water. Cook over high heat, covered, until the quinoa is soft and you can see its strings, about 15 to 20 minutes.

4. Blend it all. A food processor or blender works best here.

HEALTHY CHOCOLATE PUDDING

Do you know the difference between cacao and cocoa? In short: cacao powder hasn't been roasted and is cold-pressed to remove the fat (for cacao butter). This process means the enzymes remain active. Cocoa may look the same, but it has been roasted at high temperatures and usually contains added sugar.

This quick no-cook chocolate pudding contains only natural ingredients and is sweetened by fruit. Bonus: This recipe is freezable for up to three months. Double the ingredients and freeze half so you have some on hand whenever you or little ones crave it.

YIELD
3–4 cups (675–900 g)

INGREDIENTS
2 ripe bananas
1 large ripe avocado, pitted
8 soft pitted dates
1 tablespoon (5 g) raw
   cacao powder
1 teaspoon chia seeds
   (optional)
½ cup (120 ml) homemade
   orange juice, or other
   liquid

1. Blend it all. A food processor or blender works best here.

2. Chill for 15 minutes.

3. Serve and enjoy!

VANILLA, CHERRY, BANANA, AND OAT PUREE

Cherries are a favorite summer fruit filled with powerful antioxidants that have anticancer properties. They also contain natural melatonin, an antioxidant that helps with sleep and bodily regeneration. If you, as a sleep-deprived parent, want the benefit of cherries even when they are out of season, try tart cherry juice. This puree will keep in the refrigerator for 24 hours; the color will change but it's still edible.

YIELD
1–2 cups (225–450 g)

INGREDIENTS
3 tablespoons (15 g) oatmeal
½ cup (120 ml) milk
1 large ripe banana
½ cup (77 g) sweet cherries, pitted
½ teaspoon (2 g) vanilla powder, or 1 vanilla bean split and scraped

1. Cook the oatmeal.

2. Peel and slice the banana.

3. Blend it all. A food processor or blender works best here.

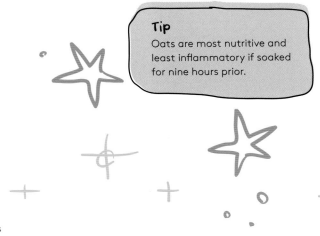

Tip
Oats are most nutritive and least inflammatory if soaked for nine hours prior.

CRANBERRY, APRICOT, AND SOUR CHERRY PUREE

This particular puree is great as is, or mixed with a little plain yogurt for a creamy, sweet, and tart breakfast! If it's too tart for your baby, substitute the sour cherries with sweet.

YIELD
2 cups (500 g)

INGREDIENTS
1 cup (100 g) fresh cranberries

3 apricots, chopped

1 cup (155 g) fresh or frozen sour cherries, pitted and chopped

1. Steam cranberries, apricots, and sour cherries together for 5 to 7 minutes, until they are soft.

2. Reserve the water from the steamer.

3. Blend the mixture in a blender until pureed. Add 1 teaspoon of reserved water at a time, if necessary, until desired consistency is achieved.

CRANBERRY, POMEGRANATE, AND GREEK YOGURT PUREE

This little combination is high in antioxidants and protein and has the needed healthy probiotics for your baby's brain to develop. All that in just one little puree—and it tastes so good!

YIELD
3 cups (750 g)

INGREDIENTS
1 cup (100 g) fresh or frozen cranberries

1 whole fresh pomegranate, seeded

1½ cups (345 g) of plain organic and grass-fed yogurt

1. Steam the cranberries for about 7 to 10 minutes, or until soft. Reserve the liquid from the steamer.

2. Puree the cranberries with the pomegranate seeds and 2 tablespoons (28 ml) of the reserved liquid. Ensure all pomegranate seeds have been fully ground. If you're not sure, run the puree through a mesh strainer.

3. Add the yogurt and blend until desired consistency is achieved.

CRAN-APPLE RAISIN PUREE

Meyer lemons are a cross between a lemon and a mandarin orange and have a more nuanced tart flavor. They are rising in popularity, so keep any eye out for them and grab some when you find them!

YIELD
2½ cups (650 g)

INGREDIENTS
1 cup (100 g) fresh
   cranberries
3 Fuji apples
¼ cup (38 g) to ½ cup (75 g)
   raisins for sweetness
Juice of half a lemon
   (Meyer lemon, if possible)

1. Steam the cranberries and apples together for 8 to 10 minutes, or until soft.

2. Add the raisins and steam for 2 additional minutes. Reserve the liquid from the steamer.

3. Puree the cranberries, apple, and raisins in a food processor with ¼ cup (60 ml) of the reserved liquid and lemon juice. Add more liquid as needed to obtain the desired consistency.

ABOUT THE AUTHORS

KAWN AL-JABBOURI is the author of *Baby Food Universe*. She runs the hugely popular Instagram account @babyfooduniverse and website www.kidsfooduniverse.com, where she posts healthy baby food and toddler food recipe ideas. She lives in Denmark with her husband and two small children.

ANNI DAULTER is a professional cook, advocate of sustainable living, and author of *Bountiful Baby Purees*, *Organically Raised: Conscious Cooking for Babies & Toddlers* (Rodale, May 2010) and *Ice Pop Joy* (Sellers). She was also the founder and operator of a fresh organic baby food company, Bohemian Baby, for three years, where she developed all recipes and branding for the company. Her food was sold to all the top celebrity babies including the children of Gwyneth Paltrow, Adam Sandler, Christy Turlington, Stevie Wonder, Bridget Fonda, Debi Mazar, the late Heath Ledger, Angela Bassett and many others. Bohemian Baby food was featured in more 60 articles and was sold in local Whole Foods stores. Anni has since ceased production and writes cookbooks with a healthy focus for families. Her website, Conscious Family Living, can be found at www.annidaulter.com. She lives in Pennsylvania.

KELLY GENZLINGER, C.N.C., C.M.T.A., has dedicated many years to the study of nutrition and foods effects within the human body. She is a traditional-foods advocate in her community and is dedicated to promoting wellness for her children, family, and nutritional clients. She is co-author of *Super Nutrition for Babies*. Also a speaker and certified nutritional consultant, Kelly is proud to have changed the lives of countless children and adults with her teachings, guidance, and counsel related to whole, real, traditional foods. Her first book, *Sugar...Stop the Addiction*, addressed the national crisis of excessive sugar consumption. She has been a featured speaker at wellness symposiums and a guest on cable shows such as Diabetes Countdown and The Bottom Line. She resides in Michigan.

KATHERINE ERLICH, M.D., is a board-certified pediatrician and mother of two who practices out of one of the largest holistic medical center in the Midwest. She is co-author of *Super Nutrition for Babies*. Prior to starting her now thriving pediatric practice, she spent over a decade in a busy, conventional pediatric practice where she gained extensive clinical experience. Currently, at Healing the Whole Child, PLLC, Dr. Erlich guides her patients to better health through an individualized medical approach, integrating nutrition, holistic philosophies and traditional medicine. Dr. Erlich has been instrumental in creating her school district's Wellness Committee, featured on the news, and has authored articles printed in several publications. She lives in Michigan.

INDEX